Born to Brawl

Gaining a Fighter's Edge in Business and Life

By Julian Rivera

BORN TO BRAWL:
GAINING A FIGHTER'S EDGE IN BUSINESS AND LIFE

ISBN: 978-1-7355185-0-3

Manufactured in the United States of America
First printing November 2020

Table of Contents

Preface

"Everybody is selling something" is a phrase often heard. I even find myself saying it from time to time. Usually I will say it when someone expresses their unwillingness to be looked at as a salesperson. I'll say "everybody is selling something" because it's true. Anytime there is an exchange of goods or services, or even a simple agreement, a sale has been made. When I first became a professional sales person, I had to grasp this concept to become comfortable with my profession. That wasn't easy in the beginning, especially during the first six months of my sales career as an advertising salesman.

As a way to earn extra side money, I used to sell CD's of mixed hip hop music also known as "mixtape CD's." I was in a barber shop selling CD's to people waiting for their haircuts when I met a gentleman who thought I would be a good fit for the company he worked for, a small advertising company in Springfield, Massachusetts. Soon after meeting him and selling him a few CD's, I interviewed with that company. I was offered the job on the spot, and off I went, on to my new career as professional salesperson.

This was business to business selling, something totally different from selling CD's on the street. My first two weeks on the job was mostly acquiring some sales training and product knowledge. My training consisted of role playing specific sales scripts to practice with my managers in the sales office before going out and speaking with real customers. Once I got out in the field selling to actual business owners, I realized that the real training had only just begun. It took me 6 months of cold calling, face to face conversations, and a lot of rejection, before I finally "figured it out." I even had thoughts of finding another career before I ultimately decided that I needed to make it work, and more importantly, that I could make it work. I used a simple approach. The more time I spent in front of people, the more likely I was to make a sale. Therefore after a few months of hearing a lot of "no's," I doubled down on my efforts. I arrived to work earlier, stayed later, and made more calls. This extra effort coupled with a refinement of my sales technique led to my initial success in selling. Within a year I had created a new version of myself with regards to professional selling. I became a top sales producer, and I then went on to become a top sales producer with multiple companies.

Fast forward a decade. I walked into a Mixed Martial Arts gym to take my first class in Brazilian Jiu-Jitsu. I had no idea what to expect, only that I wanted to try it and see how I liked it. My first class consisted of trying a few techniques which the instructor demonstrated, then watching as the students did some live sparring. By my second class, I was participating in the live sparring, and was hooked on the art of Brazilian Jiu-Jitsu. I found it to be extremely challenging yet unequivocally rewarding. Again I used a simple approach. The more time I spent on the mats, the more proficient I became at applying techniques. Therefore, I began my journey as a Brazilian Jiu-Jitsu practitioner.

I met others during my Martial Arts quest who inspired me in different ways. Some were dedicated to becoming professional fighters. Others were hobbyists with families and children who dedicated sufficient time to their training, despite their financial and familial obligations. Others were people who made astonishing transformations, both physically and mentally, one day entering as shy and out of shape, then later on emerging as confident and hard-bodied individuals. In my early years practicing Brazilian Jiu-Jitsu, I was reminded of how I must have appeared when I was a brand new salesperson – uncut, raw, impressionable, and eager. In many ways those characteristics are still with me, thankfully so! As I applied what I learned in Martial Arts to my business, I noticed that I became more productive, resilient and adaptable to change. I thought about how this came to be and I came to the conclusion that it was a shift in my mind. Not only had I changed physically, but mentally I became a fighter. With this shift in mindset, I experienced more prosperity in my business and personal life.

I continue to find interconnections between what I learn in business, and what I learn in the Martial Arts. The interconnections become more pronounced with expanded accomplishment in these respective fields. I often interact with Martial Artists and Entrepreneurs who have experienced tremendous success. I wrote this book in order to unveil the correlation between fighting and business. I interviewed multiple champion Martial Artists, some of which are also Entrepreneurs, and I consulted with them on the topic of achievement. "Born to Brawl: Gaining a Fighter's Edge in Business and Life" is a compilation of what champion fighters think, say, and do in order to be champions. My goal with this book is that you take these ideas and use them to enhance your business and personal life. Applied consistently, the suggestions in this book are intended to provide you with the means to experience continuous fortune. I hope you enjoy reading and then applying what you learn in this book.

Introduction

Have you ever wondered how a professional fighter thinks, and what makes fighters do what they do? If so, you are not alone. To voluntarily participate in a physical confrontation, where initially there is no perceived threat, is a uniquely human trait. It's fascinating if you think about it. Whether amateur or professional, what goes through the mind of a fighter is something I often think about, as it is probably one of the most intense experiences a human being can have, and in this case voluntarily. This intensity defines life in many ways to me, as it condenses all aspects of life into one event, a fight. The emotions experienced, along with the unpredictability, can make a fight an exhilarating event. Other animals have confrontations over territory, mates, food and such, but these are usually spur of the moment impulsive confrontations, and usually directly affect life and death, therefore the animals are simply reacting. Even when most other animals "play fight," it usually appears to be spur of the moment. To actually get into a mutually consented fight, at an agreed upon venue, at an agreed upon time, with the intent to entertain an audience, is a human phenomenon. Actively engaging in combat is something that can be seen as weird, scary, exciting, or just plain psychotic depending on the observer. Yet when you think about it, fighting is part of our lives. As a matter of fact, even within our day to day language, we often use fighting terminology such as, "I'm coming out swinging," "I've got them on the ropes," "I got knocked down but I got right back up," "Stick and move,"

"He's out for the count," "I hit him with the one two punch," "man did I dodge that one," "I need you in my corner," etc. Whether we are consciously aware of it or not, fighting is ingrained in our vocabulary. It is not a new phenomenon that fighting phrases have become part of our day to day language. Fighting has been part of our culture, as human beings, as long as we've existed on this planet. Furthermore the "fight or flight" response is still encoded in our DNA as our physiology often displays. Sometimes just thinking about a confrontation can be enough to raise the heart rate and alter breathing. Before a big business meeting, an interview, or an important sales call people may even experience an adrenalin rush similar to the rush a fighter gets before a fight. That's our body's way of keeping us alert and ready for action. Let's take a concentrated look at the similarities between fighting and business. We can learn from fighters and use those similarities to our benefit. We need to understand how to harness the energy of the situation and "win the fight." By our very nature, we as humans, are born fighters.

I was introduced to professional fighting at an early age. My Mom and Dad are both boxing fans and I have a few uncles who are retired boxers on my mom's side of the family. I naturally became a boxing fan as well. Growing up in the Bronx, I had to learn a thing or two about protecting myself. I credit most of what I learned about fighting as a kid to my mom, dad, and my uncle. My mom and dad taught me that it was my right and my duty to stand up for myself. My uncle, Victor Sanchez, taught me how to do it. He taught me a few basic boxing techniques when I was a boy, and the little skill I developed back then served me well. I also used to slap box and wrestle with my friends, and king of the hill was a favorite game of ours. For those that don't know what king of the hill is, it's basically kids wrestling one another on a hill until there is one kid left standing at the top of the hill victorious, and as you can imagine it's a game that often gets rough. Also, it was not uncommon for some kids in my neighborhood to come outside with boxing gloves, and we would pair up and go at it with each other, one on one. We'd have a neighborhood boxing match while onlookers would cheer us on as they formed a circle around us creating a modified boxing ring. My parents enrolled me in Karate, and I took a few classes here and there, but never stayed consistent with it as a child/adolescent. I enjoyed various sports and baseball was the one that stuck with me for the majority of my childhood and into my early twenties. I had the tremendous opportunity of playing baseball in college, which was an amazing experience. I am still a baseball fan, and I thoroughly enjoy the game of baseball to this day, although I rarely play anymore.

Later as an adult in my early thirties, I decided to get back into shape after a few years of being out of shape. I was working long hours as an advertising salesman, doing fairly well financially but smoking and boozing a bit too much, plus not exercising enough, therefore I was overweight. Being a former college athlete, I had it in me to *want to* stay in shape. I would do push-ups, sit-ups, and pull-ups here and there, but the workouts became less frequent, and I gradually became less motivated to keep at it. Finally one day I just decided that I needed to get back in shape and ultimately stay in shape! I got my ass back in the gym and made the choice to stay consistent with it. However, I felt I needed something else besides lifting weights and running on a treadmill to keep me interested and stay in tip top shape. I considered Martial Arts, and like many males in my age group, I was attracted to the UFC craze. I had seen Royce Gracie handle himself against larger and stronger opponents in the UFC octagon back in the mid to late 1990s, and that memory prompted me to give Brazilian Jiu-Jitsu a try. It was one of the best decisions of my life. I almost immediately fell in love with everything about Brazilian Jiu-Jitsu and it has now led to a 10-year love affair. As I write this book, I am still in love with Brazilian Jiu-Jitsu, the physical and mental challenge, the conditioning, the competition, the comradery, everything about it. Becoming a Brazilian Jiu-Jitsu practitioner is truly one of the best decisions I ever made, and I am committed to it for the rest of my life! Now that is something I don't say often, but it goes to show the power of a passion, and I'm lucky to have found it in the amazing Martial Art of Brazilian Jiu-Jitsu.

I have had the privilege to train with several amateur and professional Mixed Martial Artists through Brazilian Jiu-Jitsu. I recently have grown interest in the striking arts (I still enjoy watching a good boxing match), and I have been training some striking in addition to the grappling based Brazilian Jiu-Jitsu. Striking is a general term for punches, kicks, elbows, knees and any other body part you can "strike" with. I primarily operate within a circle of folks who fight because they enjoy it, and it is quite ironic because they would be the last people to actually pick a fight on the street or in a bar or club, they just don't do that, generally speaking. Fighters have the propensity for violence, however, most real fighters are not violent. Almost everybody I meet within the fight community is a humble, sincere, and down to earth person. I enjoy speaking with these individuals and really appreciate their attitudes towards life. Most fighters are intelligent, articulate and thoughtful. It didn't take me long to find a correlation between the fighting arts and business, both of which I have extensive experience with. Through training martial arts I noticed various concepts that apply to life, mainly that becoming better is related to consistency, effort, and belief, more than anything else. I have also had the privilege to earn a good living as a professional salesperson and I know that being successful in business isn't necessarily due to personality or any inborn traits, but rather due to learned and acquired skills applied consistently with passion and confidence. Therefore, I believe that successful business people can learn valuable lessons from successful professional fighters. The correlation in success between fighting and business is what this book will explore in detail.

We are going to take a look at what motivates top performing professional fighters in various professional combat sports. We will gain insight into how they prepare for their defining moment, The Fight. We are also going to explore what motivating factors and mindsets these fighters portray, and how these can be used in other parts of life, specifically in business. We will explore the winning characteristics of these top performing prize fighters, and help you apply these characteristics, traits, and habits to your line of work, so that you too can become a champion at your craft. These top performing fighters will help us analyze their best teachable attributes so that you can apply them to your chosen profession. Let's get ready to fight. By doing so you will gain the fighter's edge. After all, you are born to brawl!

Chapter 1: Win the Mental Game First

Johnny Lopez, Reality Fighting Mixed Martial Arts (MMA) Flyweight Champion, is a humble man by nature and truly one of the nicest people I know. Hence his MMA fight moniker "Mr. Nice Guy." He has recently attempted to change that moniker to "No More Mr. Nice Guy," but that name isn't as fitting, other than fight night, so "Mr. Nice Guy" is what most people still call him. He really is an incredibly nice individual; outside of the MMA cage that is. Inside the cage he's somewhat of a beast! Johnny teaches a kids' Brazilian Jiu-Jitsu class at Underdog MMA, the gym he trains at, and seeing him interact with the kids in his class, you would never guess that he is such a savage inside a cage. Johnny is a family man and also holds a full time job (MMA doesn't exactly pay the bills until you make it to the UFC, which is the ultimate goal for almost every MMA fighter. The UFC or Ultimate Fighting Championship is the premier organization in Mixed Martial Arts). With all that Johnny has on his plate, he still trains hard and faces tough opponents in pursuit of his MMA dream to be a world champion. He is currently ranked the #1 pro MMA flyweight in New England, the #4 pro MMA flyweight in the Northeast, and the #10 pro MMA flyweight in the country.

Johnny's chosen profession in combat sports is Mixed Martial Arts. As the name implies, Mixed Martial Arts is an amalgam of various Martial Arts disciplines in which individual fighters utilize the most effective techniques which work for them. These techniques usually come from striking arts, and ground fighting or grappling arts. For example, the striking arts may consist of all or one of various arts such as Muay Thai, Karate, and Kickboxing. The ground fighting or grappling arts may consist of all or one of various arts such as Brazilian Jiu-Jitsu, Wrestling, Judo, and Sambo. There are a multitude of other disciplines, but the ones mentioned here are all common within the Mixed Martial Arts arena.

I initially interviewed Johnny at his home in Berlin, Connecticut, right before a UFC fight night which he was hosting. Johnny was with his family and had invited a few friends over to watch the fights. We were discussing a lot of things, such as one of Johnny's upcoming fights to defend his Reality Fighting MMA Flyweight Championship Belt. I began the interview with Johnny by asking him about the mental aspect of a fight, and how this can translate to other aspects of life. Johnny explained "most of the fight is mental, 90-95%." He went on to mention that during training "mentally you have to reach your breaking point and push past it." This ability to push past his "breaking point" in training gives him the confidence he needs to know that if/when things get tough during the fight, or things are not going his way, he can persist and turn things around in his favor.

One of the techniques Johnny uses to push past the breaking point is to train striking or grappling to exhaustion, literally until he feels that he has nothing physically left, then he continues training by relying on instinct and proficiency to survive. This is a very effective technique for those willing to apply the physical stamina required. In relation to other aspects of life where physical stamina may apply such as working a full time job, being a parent, running a business etc., the ability to push past the "breaking point" can be extremely useful. For Johnny, this technique requires staying physically and mentally strong. This technique can be applied as simply as coming home from a long days' work and still finding the energy to work out, spend time with friends and family, complete a project, and run some errands. We always can do more than we think, especially if we are committed to a goal. Johnny's goal is to win the next fight. Your goal may be to get that promotion, get in shape, build a relationship, start a business, or take your business to the next level. Whatever your goal is, you sometimes need to push past the "breaking point" and do that little extra, do whatever it takes to reach your goal. When you consistently give a little extra, it becomes a habit, and done over time, it becomes your personality. This will help you accomplish more. With the goal kept firmly in mind, there is no other option than to finish the task at hand.

So what mental technique does Johnny Lopez use to push past the "breaking point," and how can you apply this to your life? I asked him this very question and he responded by saying "Staying in a positive mindset keeps the mind clearer. Don't let emotions, especially anger take over. Anger is a chaotic mind. Don't dwell on the negative, visualize a positive outcome, no matter the situation." The ability to stay positive in the face of adversity is invaluable. There is no mental technique more effective than this when you are facing a difficult situation. Think about it, if a fighter is losing a fight, what good will it do him/her to dwell on the possible negative outcome. Staying focused on the positive outcome, the outcome that the fighter wants, is the only solution and will be the catalyst the fighter needs to turn the tables in their favor. When a fighter is training, by staying focused on how he/she wants to appear, a cool collected killer, the fighter can train past exhaustion. The body will comply with what the mind sees. The same technique applies to business. If you are in the midst of a large deal, and the deal starts to head in the wrong direction, you can visualize the outcome you want and focus on that. This will help you move the deal towards your desired outcome. I admit this is a lot easier said than done, but it can be done. Remember to keep a clear mind by not letting anger, fear, or any of the negative emotions take over. It is best to cut these emotions off as soon as they appear, do not give them a chance to invade your mind. You can do this by managing your thoughts to refocus on the positive outcome. Your clear vision of the victory will keep your mind sharp and you will begin to move towards your desired result.

I was able to get Johnny to expand on his use of visualization, a technique that I find very useful because anybody can do it, but it does take practice and consistency. Johnny said, "I visualize the event with different situations, good and bad, where in the end I persevere. I believe it, and I see it." As simple as this may sound, it is a technique that requires practice as it involves focus. The power of focus can be developed by techniques such as meditation, concentrated breathing, and physical activities which require undivided attention to the task at hand. The ability to apply focus and visualization to all aspects of life will dramatically increase your productivity and results. Notice how Johnny said he visualizes different situations or scenarios, good and bad. He realizes the fight may not always go his way, yet he visualizes overcoming the challenge and persevering to win the fight. This is an extremely effective visualization technique, as it forces you to overcome adversity in your mind, and once you do this your confidence soars, knowing that you have the ability to come out on top. It is similar to creating scenes of a movie and being the hero of that movie. This mental rehearsal becomes a reality in your mind and that's the most important thing in my opinion. Seeing, and feeling the emotions of victory ensure a victorious performance. If your mind sees it, then your body will follow. When you are in the midst of battle you'll be acting as if you've been there before because you have. So now when circumstances arise, you are ready, because you have practiced overcoming adversity in your mind. You know how to deal with it because you have been there and done that.

Visualization is best practiced when you are relaxed, preferably alone, and in a quiet place. Try sitting in a comfortable position, and focus on your breathing for a few minutes. Let your breathing become steady, and relax your body more and more with every exhale. When you are in a state of total relaxation, you can start your visualization. Use your imagination to create the details of the event as you picture it. Focus on all the senses associated with the event. How does it look, feel, sound, smell, taste? Visualize what you want to happen and the feeling associated with that outcome. Really feel what you want to feel, and associate that feeling with the desired result you want to attain. End your visualization by coming back to your breathing, that is, focus on your breath. This technique should be simple and practiced as often as you'd like. It can take a few minutes or hours, it is up to you, as long as you do it consistently and you get into the feelings associated with your desired outcome. I suggest using visualization several weeks to months before an important event, and practicing it daily at the same time and location every day.

I thoroughly enjoyed Johnny's description of his techniques, so after the first interview I decided a second interview was required to get a bit more in depth with the actual processes Johnny uses in preparation for a fight. Starting with the fight camp itself, I asked Johnny to expand on some of the processes he employs. Johnny explains, "I feel that I need to be organized, I need to break it down step by step. I want a layout so that I have a guideline. I've had fights where I didn't have a layout and the level of confidence going in isn't the same. When I started training at Underdog MMA, I started to have more organization. For example, I always have kickboxing and MMA on Monday, I always have wrestling and Gi Jiu-Jitsu on Tuesday, and so on. Just having that level of organization is nice instead of just getting guys together to train with no plan, you spend a half hour just trying to figure out what you're going to do. Organization is important, and surrounding yourself with the right people is so important. I started my MMA career with two straight losses, and I thought to myself 'What the fuck?!' I felt like I was way better than that. I just didn't have the right people around me. I had a decent foundation, my cousins Justin and Robert (both MMA fighters as well), and they were always very consistent in helping me, but we all knew the same level of stuff. I needed more knowledge and organization. So getting with Russell Leak (owner and striking coach at Underdog), and the team at Underdog allowed me to see the process. I was also able to embrace the process, not only writing it out but doing it. Some of the steps are things that you may not want to do. Like I have to go run, I don't want to run, I can't eat bread, I don't want to do these things, I want to eat what I want! (laughs) But you have to take the necessary steps. It's part of the process."

Johnny went on to explain how this process he describes also helps his use of visualization. "To me, this process all leads to better visualization because if all the steps are being taken, now you are starting to see the big picture.

I'm doing this because I want this. I'm taking steps 1, 2, 3, and 4 because I know that if I want to win that fight I've got to do it."

I went on to ask Johnny how taking these steps makes the outcome he wants more real. Johnny responded, "I'll talk to Matt (Matt Bessette is Johnny's mentor and a UFC veteran), and Matt will ask me 'Ok, how do you see this one?' And then I give him a detailed answer. For instance, I'll tell him, 'Ok, I know this guy wants to clinch up with me, we're going to throw some hands, and we're going to step off the midline, then I'm going to throw some kicks and threaten him with the stand up, he'll get overzealous and go for a takedown, he's going to go into my world on the ground, and I'm going to sweep him...' And I'll break it down step by step for Matt. Most of the time even if it doesn't end the way I initially thought, a lot of that happens. So the visualization works because I was preparing with all the drills, I knew what my opponent was most likely to do and I prepared for it. I feel that once you visualize the outcome you want and you're taking the necessary steps you almost know it's going to happen. You have given yourself the best chance to win. So with that, there's no regrets. If I prepared to the fullest, I have the best team so I know I'm ready, so even if I lose I don't regret a damn thing. Because I know I did everything I could to get ready. If you go in knowing you didn't run, or didn't do the extra rounds, the picture of what you want to happen gets blurred. You become unsure and then you go in to the fight not as confident, and then you have regrets. I feel like in business you have to do the same. You have to prepare to the fullest, and the steps along the way are similar because they all contribute to the end result. If you work as hard as you can and follow the guidelines as much as you can while getting ready, you won't have any regrets, even if you fail."

Johnny Lopez argues that the more you prepare physically, the sharper image of success you will see mentally and vice versa. Johnny's philosophy is "The harder you work, the more mentally strong you become, and the more mentally strong you are, the harder you're going to work. So the physical and mental goes back and forth. They work together."

Johnny has been fighting since 2012 and almost all of his fights have been professional fights. He only had a couple of fights as an amateur and went pro in 2013. Soon after he went pro, he joined the team at Underdog Mixed Martial arts and he describes that as a pivotal moment in his career. "I was 0-2 as a pro (0 wins, 2 losses) and now I'm 11-4 (11 wins, 4 losses)." I thought that was amazing how he could turn that around. "I'm 11-2 since I've been with Underdog. I've won 9 of my last 10 fights. I'm No. 1 in New England, No. 10 in the United States (MMA Flyweight). It's better than I ever imagined. So I could retire right now and have no regrets! I do it because I love it, and I have great guys around me. The love is huge! If you do something that you love it will be easy to do some of the things that aren't so fun. Like getting ready for a Jiu-Jitsu tournament, you have to make weight and sometimes that sucks, but you love the grind." I can personally attest to this statement because I have prepared for Jiu-Jitsu tournaments, and have had to make a certain weight, train everyday with intent and purpose, and get myself physically and mentally ready to go to battle. I know what it's like to not want to go train, and even justify it be telling myself, "I can use a rest day." But then that part of me that hates regret kicks in, and I know if I don't go then I will hate myself for it, so I go train. I have successfully been able to use a system of organization and consistent preparation to get ready for competition. And I love the grind too.

Johnny then described how some people may hold themselves back and how to overcome it. He says, "A lot of people want to do Jiu-Jitsu, but they say, 'I have to go to the gym first or I have to run first for a couple of weeks to get in shape,' and that's not how it works. I tell them 'just do it man, you just have to jump in. There's no time like the present. Who cares how old or young you are. Just go after it.'"

I then asked Johnny what other aspects of life he might compare fighting to and he answered pretty quickly. He said, "Parenthood! This is a war (chuckles)!" Johnny became a father not too long ago. He has a beautiful little girl, Penelope, and he absolutely adores her. Johnny explained further, "I feel like the preparation is relative. When you have a kid, you can't afford to not have food, diapers, or not be employed and (not) have health insurance for your kid. For me, I want my kid to be taken care of. I want to provide as much as possible, and that requires preparation. Like I said, sometimes it's a war. This kid can drive me nuts! But going through the fight game and dealing with the hard times helps. I know what real hard times are, I don't want somebody mounted on top of me and smashing my face with elbows. That's a real bad time! So Penelope crying because she can't get the toy she wants, I'm able to put it in perspective, it's not so bad. Plus she's way cuter (chuckles). I feel more prepared because of being in the fight game. I feel that being involved in combat sports gets you ready for business, parenthood, the daily grind of life in general. You may not want to get up early in the morning and go to work, or you may work a night shift, and not want to work overnight, but you have goals and you have to follow the steps."

Johnny's last sentence resonated with me. I told Johnny how I understood what he was saying because of my experience in the Sales Profession. I explained to Johnny how I had been pushed out of my comfort zone when I first started sales because I was timid to speak with strangers and initiate conversations. I described how I needed a deep motivational drive to help me break out of my comfort zone. I told him that for me, that drive was my daughter. I had a picture of my baby girl on my desk at work, and I would look at that picture before, and during my cold calls to potential clients. I had a fear of the phone, but my desire to provide for my daughter drove me to pick up that phone, make calls, and schedule appointments with potential buyers. The more I did it, the better I became. I had all the motivation I needed in front of me the whole time. Eventually speaking with prospective clients on the phone became a skill that I developed and became very good at. And as I got better at it, the more I enjoyed it.

Johnny replied, "Yes I get it, now you can say you have some mastery of it, because you developed it. Maybe you didn't like it at first, but you had a goal man. And that's what I think of when I prepare, I may not want to get up and run, but I sure do want my hand raised on fight night."

I then wanted to know what Johnny had next in store, so I asked him about his immediate and long term goals with regards to MMA. He answered, "I have a few things, I'm a list maker for almost everything, daily tasks, grocery shopping, or whatever...I have to make sure I have it written out so I can see it. I have a career agenda, I feel like I will train Jiu-Jitsu until the wheels fall off, once fighting is done I'll be in the Gi all the time. A big goal is to become a Black Belt in Brazilian Jiu-Jitsu, that's high on my agenda. As far as MMA goes, I would like to defend my regional title with Reality Fighting, possibly getting a third title belt. That would be great! That would look good on my wall (chuckles). I achieved the No. 1 ranking in New England, which was a goal of mine. Now if I could get a world title, such as with CES MMA (CES MMA is a very reputable and competitive MMA organization), I would love to get the CES flyweight title and I'm ready to face any opponent for that opportunity. If I could get that I might just bow out of the MMA fight game. That's the vision I see."

Johnny paused for reflection and then continued. "I had it set up where I fought in November 2018 for CES, and I won that fight. And then I fought in January, but January was supposed to be a Reality Fighting title defense against Jose Lugo, but he pulled out of the fight. I ended up fighting Johnny Campbell, but my goal was to fight Lugo in January, and retain the title, and CES had already been talking with me about fighting for a flyweight championship, and I planned to do that after the Lugo fight. But there are turns in the road. I kept my record sharp by winning the fight with Johnny Campbell, and I had planned to jump back into a fight with Jose Lugo, but now my knee was recently injured. So to me there are bumps in the road, but I'm still on the path, it's not like I veered off so far. I just take this as a little bump in the road. Right now I'm focusing on the next two to three fights, and we'll go from there. But regardless, I have no regrets. Life is good."

I believe Johnny's goals are realistic with regards to the fight game, he's accomplished a lot, and he has several more accomplishments ahead of him. I let him know and just such, and he thanked me, then he said it one more time "no regrets."

There is no doubt that Johnny's ability to stay positive and keep his mind clear will serve him well. These attributes have already helped him become Reality Fighting Flyweight Champion and well on his way to earning more championship titles. I truly believe that his positive attitude has helped him most in times of adversity. His ability to look at the positive opens his mind to opportunities that would otherwise be invisible from a pessimistic viewpoint. His positivity gives him a mental edge which has helped him in his fight career and in life. He continues on a steady climb to the top of the Nation's MMA elite. Since the initial interview, Johnny went on to win several fights for CES MMA, which are aired on live television, with hopes to fight for the CES world championship title. He has fought and won in Bellator MMA which has moved him up in the nationwide rankings in his division. He also fights to retain the Reality Fighting Flyweight Champion title. So don't let the nickname "Mr. Nice Guy" fool you; there's nothing nice when you get in the MMA cage with him. He is a relentless fighter with a killer instinct. When it's fight night, Johnny Lopez earns the name "No More Mr. Nice Guy."

I continue to surround myself with people like Johnny Lopez. I suggest you do the same. Surround yourself with positive people that you can root for, and that will root for you. This is paramount because that energy is contagious. Strive to have a positive outlook on life because this will give you the best outcome in any given situation. It is not easy by any means, but it is important. Try clearing your mind of anger, frustration, fear, and doubt. You can do this by focusing on the present moment, realizing that the past is done and the future doesn't exist, there's only the present. Use the present to calm yourself; focus on your breathing and use this calm energy to create the outcome you want. Do this in a situation where you have every right to be upset, and you will perform magic because you will astound yourself at how you can better manage the situation. Even if your anger is justified you must channel that anger, and you can do this by clearing your head first. It may take a few minutes to do this, I know this is usually the case with me. However when you are able to breathe properly, lower your heart rate and clear your mind, you will marvel at the results you can accomplish. Remember what Johnny said, "Anger is a chaotic mind." Don't fall victim to your own emotions. Staying calm and focused in the face of adversity will allow you to win the battle in your mind first, and that's where it matters the most.

Win the Mental Game First – Key Points:

- Test the limits, Keep Pushing the "breaking point" in your training, or whatever actions are required to reach your goal. Testing yourself is the only way to grow.
- Protect your positive mind. Remember that anger clouds your judgment. Staying positive keeps your mind clear and productive.
- Use visualization to rehearse attaining the outcome you desire. Since adversity will arise, picture overcoming adversity in your visualizations.
- Develop a visualization ritual and add it to your training regimen.
- Talk through your situation with someone you trust. Describe the event, using your imagination to create a dynamic scenario with the outcome you desire.
- Preparation can never be underestimated. The better prepared you are the stronger your mental state will be when it counts.
- Embrace the grind. Training can be tough at times. Know that your success will be that much sweeter.

Chapter 2: Prepare and Persist

Matt Bessette, CES MMA Featherweight World Champion and UFC veteran athlete, granted me time to interview him. I was able to ask him about what motivates him when it comes to preparation and persistence. I believe preparation and persistence are what has attributed most to Matt's success and longevity in the fight game. Being a personal witness to Matt's training camp and a Brazilian Jiu-Jitsu training partner of his, I know the amount of time and dedication Matt has put into developing himself as a world class MMA fighter.

At the time of this writing, Matt Bessette has 30-plus fights under his belt. He is ranked the No. 1 pound for pound MMA fighter in the Northeast. I must note that this interview was also done before Matt's UFC contract. To start off the interview I asked Matt a very general question, "why do you fight?" Matt stated that he has been asked that question *countless* times and that his answer has actually changed over time. He states that at this point in his career, at 32 years old, his answer is very clear and concise. Matt said, "I fight to get in to the UFC." The Ultimate Fighting Championship, or UFC, is the pinnacle of MMA fighting where contests and notoriety is concerned. I liken the UFC to the major leagues in any other sport. There are several MMA organizations, but most of them are minor league compared to the UFC. In my opinion, the closest thing to the UFC is Bellator MMA, which is gaining some traction and attracting some of the top contenders in Mixed Martial Arts. However, the UFC still reigns supreme in terms of recognition and talent.

Matt goes on to say that in addition to his reason for fighting he does not necessarily fight for other people. He fights for himself and for what he knows he can accomplish. He explains that during his most recent fight at the writing of this book he took a hard loss. It was his UFC Contender Series appearance and his shot at getting a UFC contract, his dream. Matt says, "I broke my thumb on my right hand throwing the first punch that I landed that night...I trained for 10 years for this one moment, I finally get it, and I fucking break my finger right away. If you're constantly asking yourself why, you'll never get it. The only answer is *it happens*. You have to be satisfied with, not the accomplishment, but everything you've done to get to that point."

I expressed to Matt that what I heard was him referring to "the journey" since I consider myself on "the journey" with Brazilian Jiu-Jitsu. You hear Martial Artists refer to "the journey" over and over again, but when you actually do Martial Arts, you get it. Martial Arts really is a journey because there is no end to it. Matt went on to say, "Yeah, if we're speaking as cliché as possible it is 'the journey,' and you don't understand it until you're in it. All of the heartache and day to day grind, that's what molds you. It's not about what you accomplished at the end of the day, it's what you did to get there." I feel it is takes a courageous person to make a statement like Matt did. He didn't make excuses for his recent loss, he didn't say it's okay to lose. He just stated that he is being molded by the grind and he will continue to grind. In that statement I see grit, determination and persistence!

I asked Matt how much his goals scare him, and he exclaimed, "They fucking frighten me! If your goals don't scare you they're not big enough…failure is giving up, if you refuse to give up on yourself then you never fail."

Matt goes on to say that "the fact that you took the steps to finally get to that point. To make sure that you do everything at the beginning and end of each day to further yourself in your career, life, etc. That's what makes you a successful person."

I went on to ask Matt what advice he'd give to a newbie, someone just starting a career/profession. He said that he thinks he did the right thing to start by finding people that had been there before him, and people that could put him on the right path. Matt goes on to explain "I myself had Kipp Kolar who is the president of NAGA and Reality Fighting. I didn't have a manager until my 10th fight and out of my 30 fights I only had a manager for five of them. So knowing somebody in this day and age with anything you're doing is super important. My dad used to tell me that knowing somebody is half the battle, as much as you don't want to hear that. Through school you worked your butt off for that degree, and what if you get that 4.0 and you're up for a job against someone who got the 2.4 but the other guy knows somebody and then he gets the job. Sometimes it's about who you know, it's just the way it is. If I was to do it again I would say to myself who do I need to know to get to where I need to be?"

I asked Matt what kind of networking he would use – i.e. social networking, in person, etc. Matt says, "I use any and everything. I'm big on in-person because you don't really get to know anybody unless you actually look them in the eye and talk to them. But even social media, the smallest amount of networking will help." I asked if he was comfortable reaching out to someone he doesn't know, and he says he would be, and even if you're not, you better be, because sometimes it's about who you know.

I then asked Matt, "What do you do to mentally prepare for a fight?" Matt responded by saying "I dance with the girl who brought me to the dance...if the blueprint's there, don't try anything crazy." He reflects on a technique he used to help him prepare for a fight he had by saying, "One fight, when I had to fight Diego Nunes, I was scared. I was scared not because of what he could do, but I questioned 'am I what everybody thinks I am?' Am I able to go out there and do it? So I'm by myself 20 minutes before the fight, in the bathroom, and I just started talking to myself in the mirror. I ask myself, what are you afraid of? I tell myself everything I'm afraid of. 'I'm afraid getting knocked out in front of my friends, I'm afraid of not being the winner that everybody wants me to be, I'm afraid of this that and the next thing'...I was just able to verbalize these things and it helped! I left the bathroom feeling like somebody else other than me knows this, the mirror knows this, the other guy knows this, and somebody else knows this. And I was able to go out there and do my thing." I asked if he felt by verbalizing it he got it off his chest and diminish its power, and he shook his head stating "Yeah, at that point is wasn't even a thought anymore." I commended Matt on this technique he used before the fight stating that this was a technique I had not heard of yet.

Verbalizing your fears allows you to acknowledge them. After acknowledging the fear you can verbalize that the fear has no power, you have conquered it, because by stating it you can follow up with a statement that negates it just as easily. Have the courage to state your fears, acknowledge them, and put them out there. I feel that you must also have the courage to state how your fear is not real and that you trust your instincts and training to take over. Verbalizing is a part of self-talk and it is a powerful tool when used correctly. Use your words to empower you. I feel that verbalizing scenarios to play out with your desired result can work for most jitters or anxiety before a competitive event, whether it be business or sport. It worked for Matt, that's for sure – he won the fight!

I asked Matt if he had any rituals he always followed before a fight. He was hesitant to come up with any, rather stating that "sometimes I tried to follow a ritual, but it didn't work out (the ritual), and I'm thinking 'what's gonna happen?!' and I end up smashing the guy anyway." He stated the thing that matters most is preparation, then when you get in there chance comes into play. I eluded to there being a lot of variables and he agreed. I liken these variables to variables in life. The preparation allows you to go with the flow and adapt, rather than react. Preparation is a word Matt refers to a lot. He absolutely believes in preparation wholeheartedly. I've seen some of Matt's preparation before a fight and it is insane. I asked Matt how many times a week he trains before a fight and he said, "Usually twice a day six days a week. It can be a combination of striking, jiu-jitsu, shadowboxing, sprints etc. It can be easy or difficult depending on how I'm feeling. If I'm feeling really good, I'm going to bust my ass all day. If I feel like junk, I'm still going to train, but it's going to be more of a rehab workout."

I then asked Matt if during his shadowboxing sessions, he visualizes himself in the fight that he's preparing for. He replied, "Sometimes, if it's closer to a fight. Other times I listen to some hot rap music like Paradox BX (he laughs at the plug he gave me since I made a fight song for him under the rap moniker Paradox BX; you can check it out at *https://youtu.be/ygZLXT8yV_s*). I listen to some hot rap music and just move with the beat, move and let my mind relax. I may have a fight in six weeks but tomorrow I got a tough striking session so I just have to get ready for that and loosen up."

I asked Matt how he felt about the preparation for a fight translating to other parts of his life. He said, "It translates to everything. Say the fight is June 1st, and today is January 1st, and I'm preparing every single day to the fullest, mentally and physically to be the best possible person on June 1st. If I do that, I am 100% going to be the person I need to be. Like we were talking about before, two times a day six days a week are just my physical training sessions. And then if I'm not physically training you better believe that I'm on YouTube, that I'm buying books, that I'm reading, that I'm visualizing. It's an all-day thing. There's no resting. If you've got goals, if you want to succeed, there's sleep, but there's no resting."

I asked Matt what advice he would give a business person going into a big meeting. He said, "You can go into the meeting thinking you're going to lose, and odds are you're right, because you thought you were. If you go into the meeting thinking you're going to kill it and you're confident in your speech, confident in what you know, and confident in your delivery with everything, you're going to do great. If you believe it, you're going to do great! A fight is different because anything can happen at any moment. Realistically, this is not a fight, no one is going to try and punch you in the face, and you know what you have to do. The only thing that's going to stop you from succeeding is your own mind. Confidence."

We discussed how the things that matter most are the people that are close to you and because they will be there no matter what, nothing else is important. I went on to suggest that this mindset leads to a level of confidence that allows you to take on any challenge. Matt explained "confidence and happiness are two things that should propel you to whatever person you want to be in life. You're in that business meeting, and you've got 500 people looking at you, and you realize, 'I don't know any of these people, I'm here for me.' Just relax and just be. Everybody already knows you're on stage for a reason. Clearly they think you're awesome. So just be awesome. The only person that stops you from being as awesome as everybody already thinks you are, is you."

Since the time of this interview Matt was approached again by the UFC. He then signed a three-fight deal with the UFC, achieving his dream of becoming a UFC fighter.

Prepare and Persist – Key Points:

- Your goals should fucking frighten you! If your goals don't scare you they aren't big enough.
- Make connections. Actively seek people that are like-minded and goal-oriented, especially if they are already doing what you want to do.
- Verbalize your triumph. What are you afraid of? Good. Now state how you will overcome it.
- Preparation is sacred. It is the most important factor which determines success. Treat it as such.
- Confidence starts with your thoughts. Stay focused on what you want to have happen.
- Just be awesome! Get lost in the moment when your performance counts. Recognize that this is what you worked so hard for. Let it flow.

Chapter 3: Recognize the Opportunity

Jose "Rated R" Rivera is a professional boxer with an interesting career path. Jose Rivera's pro boxing record at the time of this writing is 4 wins, 1 loss, 3 KO's. Jose trains out of Hartford Boxing Center in Hartford, Connecticut. Jose was a shy kid and somewhat of an introvert while growing up. He always had an interest in fighting, but in his teen years he was too shy to seek out a fight gym. He started training MMA through a friend of his, Manny, who introduced him to Kipp Kolar, the same person that gave Matt Bessette his start in Mixed Martial Arts. Kipp owns and operates NAGA (North American Grappling Association), a global grappling organization, and he also owns and operates Reality Fighting, an MMA organization that has a solid foothold in the Northeastern United States. Jose decided to take on the challenge to step up and not be shy anymore. So in his early twenties, Jose started training in "Kipp's Basement," which became a training facility for many up and coming fighters. Jose won his first amateur MMA fight at Mohegan Sun casino by 2nd round knockout. The Mohegan Sun fight helped Jose decide that fighting was his true calling.

I asked Jose how he transitioned from MMA to Boxing, and he explained, "I always was a striker, a lot of the MMA guys had strong grappling backgrounds, and I felt it was easier for them to transition to MMA. I always liked to strike, so once the guys I fought got tagged they wanted to take it to the ground, which wasn't my strongest area. I lost two amateur MMA fights in a row by decision because of not being able to defend the takedowns. That drove me to train harder in my ground game, jiu-jitsu and wrestling. Soon after, I won three straight fights by guillotine choke (the guillotine choke is a common submission wrestling choke with a front headlock around your opponent's neck, cutting off the arteries, and strangling him/her, causing them to "tap out" or risk passing out). I proved that I could be a well-rounded MMA fighter, but I still had a passion for boxing. I saw that there was a boxing event that gave the winner a belt, and that caught my eye. I went to the boxing gym and told them I wanted to fight for that belt. They asked me if I had trained and I told them I was an MMA fighter. They explained I needed a boxing gym to represent me and to train in order to fight for the belt. I told them I was ready and asked, 'Where do I sign?' They thought I was crazy. They signed me up and the next day I went to the gym and sparred the best amateur 165 pounder at the gym, which is my weight class. I dropped him three times and he quit boxing that day. That's how I found out I had some real talent for boxing and my coaches were really impressed. That's how I started boxing. Then I fought that first fight and got the belt."

I asked Jose about accomplishing his goal of winning that first boxing tournament and receiving that first belt. I asked Jose which played the bigger role, his will or his talent. Jose responded, "I think it was a little bit of both. I really, really wanted that belt (laughs). I trained really hard and sparred a lot. I only really had like two months to prepare for that boxing match. It was here in Hartford, Conn. There were a lot of people at the show who didn't know I boxed but knew me from MMA so they were cheering for me. It was my first boxing fight, I was really nervous, more nervous than when I stepped in the cage to fight MMA. First round I didn't do great because I felt people watching and cheering for me, which made me nervous. But then second round I calmed down, and I got a second round uppercut stoppage to win the fight."

I loved this story because it speaks to Jose's will to win and his preparation. Furthermore he explained that he was nervous, he actually used that word, *nervous*, a lot. Most of us might also be nervous in that situation, and what Jose did was confront that feeling. He felt the nervous feeling acknowledged that it was there, then persevered mentally and let his training carry him to victory. This took courage because even though he felt nervous, he still moved forward towards his goal. Being nervous is normal. It's what you do with that nervous energy that makes the difference between victory and defeat. Properly channeled energy, combined with focus and action, will produce the outcome you desire.

I asked Jose how he sets his goals when it comes to fighting. He replied, "I want to get better and push myself harder every day. I see a lot of progression in my skills and my boxing career right now. They're talking about giving me a shot at a New England professional belt, which will move me up in the ranks. This next fight is really important; I'm fighting Troy Artis. He's fought a lot of undefeated professionals, and they haven't been able to stop him. He's a tough opponent, and I feel like this will be a great fight. I am training hard for it. If I get this win, they might give me a shot at that belt, so that's really my goal right now, is to get a shot at the New England belt."

I appreciated how Jose started out his fight career as an MMA fighter and then transitioned into boxing. He could have been a decent MMA fighter, but being a striker (someone who is adept at punches, kicks, knees, elbows etc.) and having a passion for that part of the sport, made him pursue boxing instead. He was not afraid to switch his path, something far too many of us are not willing to do. He felt that his talents were best suited for boxing and he was able to go down that new path without hesitation once he saw the opportunity. He has pursued boxing with everything he has and has not looked back. This is a lesson we can all learn from. The door may open, but it is up to you to walk through it.

I asked Jose what attributes a fighter needs to win a fight. Jose says "To win a fight you need skills. But even more than skills you need conditioning, because without conditioning you can't perform. I focus on being in the best shape, all around, running, strong arms, legs, whole body conditioning."

Conditioning in fighting is often what separates champions from contenders. The way Jose described conditioning as total body conditioning is what has made him more balanced and well-rounded as a fighter. This balance is important because you need strength in all aspects of your body and mind in fighting, just like you need balance in all aspects of business and life. If you are strong in some areas, yet need improvement in others, make sure you enhance the areas that need improvement. For example if you are a salesperson who is great at establishing rapport, yet weak at closing the sale, then work on closing the sale. You should not rely on one skill if you want to be considered elite, no more than a champion boxer relies on one physical trait, or one punch for that matter, to beat every opponent. The work you put in to balance your skillset will reap rewards for the length of your career.

I then asked Jose what goes on in his head during a fight, especially that first fight. He said "Every fight is different. There are different emotions and feelings for every fight and every fighter. My first fight I was so nervous when I was getting my hands wrapped that I wanted to quit right there, but it was just mind tricks. I got in the zone a bit when I heard the crowd cheering for me. Once I was in there I felt like I got locked in a cage and I saw my opponent looking at me like he wanted to kill me so I was like 'I'm gonna die!' (laughs). But it's either you or him so you have to man up and let your cardio and talent do the work." Jose went on to explain how he begins to get in the fight. "I'm really a calm person so I feel like I have to get hit (first) to go in fight mode. I go in and spar but once I get hit I know it's a fight and I know it's time to put in the work and do what we came here to do."

I asked Jose to tell me the hardest thing he had to overcome before or during a fight. Jose said "There was one fight that my 9-year-old son, Jordan Rivera, was at. His mom never took him to my fights because she thought it was too hard for him to watch. So one of my fights he actually got to go, and just watching (him) in the crowd gave me watery eyes. I had to look away and toughen up. I told myself I have to do this for a better future for me and for him." I acknowledged the kind of motivation that seeing his son must've brought him, and asked Jose what else motivated him. He said, "Just me, my family, and everybody that supports me, that's all the motivation right there. And I just want to be great at what I do."

I asked Jose what advice he might give to someone looking to get into the fight game, a question I feel is also applicable to anyone looking to get into any "game," especially business. Jose replied, "It's not for everybody. This is a hard sport; it takes a lot of sacrifice and dedication. My advice to them is if you're thinking about it, don't wait. I wish I would've started earlier. I feel like I started a little late, but it's really never too late for anything, it depends on how much work you put in. So if they're already training, work hard, stay motivated and push on."

I recalled a conversation I had with Jose after one of Johnny Lopez' MMA fights at Mohegan Sun Casino in Connecticut. Jose told me that he was quiet and reserved and that fighting has helped him to be more vocal. I asked Jose what advice he would give to someone who is quiet by nature, works at a company, and has good ideas, but is too shy to share them. Jose gave his advice, "I feel like it's all in your head, overcome that fear and just try it." Jose recalled a time when he was 14 and went to a gym and turned around because he was too shy to walk in. He admits this regret and lets it fuel him for his success now and in the future. Jose continued, "If you have great ideas seek out the right people and share them. You never know what those ideas can accomplish. Start right now. Don't waste another day."

The tenacity Jose demonstrates is universally accepted as one of the key elements to success. Jose has the passion to succeed. As soon as he decides on a goal he has the dedication to follow through by putting in the necessary work to achieve his goal. Even though Jose started training later in life than the typical professional boxer, he is determined to make a name for himself in the boxing profession. In his fight against the tough opponent, Troy Artis, Jose lost by decision. Although he lost that fight he did not try to justify the loss or make excuses. He went right back to the gym to train and is continuing to train hard in his pursuit of attaining the New England championship belt. Jose has continued moving towards his goal. With his tenacity and dedication to be the best, Jose "Rated R" Rivera is a name to remember. There is no doubt in my mind, or in Jose's mind, that he is a champion in the making.

Since the Troy Artis fight, Jose Rivera has been on a winning streak. He is continuing his training and successfully pursuing his professional fight career. His most recent win was by referee stoppage (TKO), and he is scheduled to fight again in a few weeks. One thing that Jose didn't emphasize in his interview but that I noticed about him is his work ethic. He never stops training. He is constantly in gyms cross training and building his knowledge base in his profession of boxing. He has trained internationally in dedication to his quest for expertise. Jose is a true life learner, having started his pro boxing career later in life than others (he started in his early twenties) has been a blessing in my opinion. He has a keen sense of urgency and thirst for boxing education. He is determined and energized knowing that his window of opportunity is now. His talent for the sport can only take him so far. The rest is up to the amount of work he puts in based on the wisdom he gains, and Jose puts a lot of work in. He's a blue collar, East Coast hard ass who is intent on his career, meeting people, training, taking fights, and making things happen. I often see him posting positive content on social media, keeping his fans current on his progress. He's taking action to follow his dream, and that speaks volumes in achievement. I believe it is universally accepted that action is necessary to achieve success. Jose "Rated R" Rivera is the epitome of that action.

Recognize the Opportunity – Key Points:

- Sometimes an opportunity presents itself in a subtle way, if your instincts tell you to go for it, listen and go forward. As long as your new path is progressive, keep moving and don't look back.
- Feel the nerves, gather your courage, and move forward. Channel the nerves with focus and action. You may even surprise yourself when you trust and believe in your ability.

- Train all the time. Champions work harder than the runner-up. Think "If I'm not training, the competition is."
- Find your motivation. Family, loved ones, even enemies, or those you want to prove wrong. A strong source of motivation can provide the fuel to push you to do whatever it takes.
- Start now. If you want to achieve a goal, advance your career, or start a business, whatever it may be, stop thinking and take action!

Chapter 4: Stay Determined

Leonardo Delgado is a Brazilian Jiu-Jitsu 2nd degree Black Belt, receiving his black belt in December 2011. Leo is originally from Rio de Janeiro, where he studied philosophy and business administration. In Rio, he worked as a marketing manager in a multinational company before deciding to pursue his passion of being a full time Brazilian Jiu-Jitsu competitor and instructor. Leo left Brazil for the United States where he now instructs and competes full time. Leo is a valued member of the Soul Fighters Brazilian Jiu-Jitsu competition team. Leo competes in Brazilian Jiu-Jitsu year round and he enjoys competing in the Gi (think martial arts kimono), and No-Gi (think rash guard or T-shirt and shorts). Leo competes mainly in the IBJJF (International Brazilian Jiu-Jitsu Federation) tournaments, which are considered by many to hold the highest standard in BJJ competition. His major accomplishments in Brazilian Jiu-Jitsu include the following championships, Pan American No-Gi, Brazilian Nationals No-Gi, American Nationals No-Gi, Worlds No-Gi, South American Championship in the Gi, and third place in the World Masters Gi (2015).

Leo started training in Brazilian Jiu-Jitsu when he was 14 and explained that when he first started training back in Rio, "People would see Jiu-Jitsu guys as brawlers and troublemakers, so Jiu-Jitsu was frowned upon. My parents never supported me that way; they came from a really old school generation where you had to go to school to become a doctor or lawyer or join the military. I always did Jiu-Jitsu and continued doing it, but I walked a different way professionally. I went to college and studied philosophy and business administration and worked a bunch of jobs, but my biggest job was with a tobacco company. I joined as a trainee and became a marketing manager. But Jiu-Jitsu was always my passion, I kept going on and off until it got to the point that I decided to do Jiu-Jitsu full time which is what I always wanted to do." I had to assume that Leo was happier, and he agreed with a laugh saying, "Definitely, no question about it!" Leo quit his job in 2013 and opened a business which gave him more time to train Jiu-Jitsu and then in 2014 a friend urged him to go to the United States and become a Brazilian Jiu-Jitsu professor. He thought about it and decided to give it a go. He remembers thinking "It's now or never," and he believed he made the right choice. His extraordinary accomplishments and solid reputation within the Jiu-Jitsu community are a testament to his decision.

I asked Leo one of the most important questions I could ask a fighter when it comes to finding a correlation between fighting and business, I asked him, "What drives you?" Leo said, "Ever since I was little I started thinking about this, what drives me is...I know it sounds cliché, but what drives me is to try and be a better version of myself every day. I made a couple mistakes when I was younger that I regret a lot and since that phase of my life I told myself I need to be a better person, I need to try and do something better every day. In Jiu-Jitsu, in life, in business, I want to be better, I want to accomplish things. I'm pretty competitive so competition is a big part of it for me. Even in business every time I had a sales campaign I wanted to be first and for my team to win the prizes, I'd want to be top five, top two, be the first. I don't want to prove anything to anybody I just want to make sure that I'm being competitive and working to stay competitive through the times." I asked Leo if he felt like he was basically competing with himself and he agreed "yes all the time."

My next question was a two-parter. I asked Leo how he set his goals and then how he reassesses them when necessary. Leo eloquently answered, "I set my goals, and I split them into short-, middle-, and long-term goals. For example, a short-term goal would be 'This week I have to train three times a day every day.' A middle-term goal would be 'In two months I have to be 175 lbs. for that competition.' And a long-term goal would be, this one's for real, 'I want to have every major title to the end of my career. I want to be a world champion in the Gi, which I'm not yet, I want to be a Pan Ams champion in the Gi which I'm not yet. So every major competition like Europeans, Pan Ams, Worlds, and the Nationals, I want to have a gold medal from each one of those tournaments through the end of my career.' So I try to split them into short-, middle, and long-term goals." He went on to explain, "My long-term goals probably are not going to change...Usually I reassess the short term goals often. Every few months I will look at whether or not the goals have been accomplished and if not, new goal! So if I didn't get something, I look at what I need to change to get what I want. It's really intense man, my mind is busy. My long term goals probably won't change. I want a gym, not just to make a few bucks and have a living, no I want to create an army. I want 300 people in that gym, an army of kids, and an army of adults. I want to take the team to competitions and help the team grow and make the Soul Fighters name bigger in the Jiu-Jitsu scene. I want to produce world champions, that's my vision. So that is the kind of thing that doesn't change, when you have a desire, when you have a dream."

I then focused the discussion on competition. I acknowledged Leo for competing year round, traveling all over the United States to compete. Leo stated, "I try to stay active as much as I can because it's part of what I do. I'm very competitive, and I want to tell myself that I can keep doing that. Some people tell me to compete at Masters 2 which is my age group, but I want to compete in Masters 1 (a lower age group). I want to keep telling myself that I'm still able compete with younger people and I'm still on top of my game (laughs). But I'm not a fool, once I feel that I'm not on top of my game anymore I'll feel it's time to move forward. But yeah, competition is a big part of my life."

I respect Leo for his competitive edge, and he is a beast in competition. I knew that Leo could provide some raw insight into what a business person could do with his knowledge. With that in mind I asked him, "With a background in business, what similarities do you see between business and fighting?" He replied, "I believe the biggest one is the preparation. When you are going to a meeting you have to have everything prepared – your numbers, what you want to negotiate, everything. So I believe in preparation. I believe in hard work. I believe that hard work trumps talent. I want to be the hardest worker in the room. I fully believe in preparation in business, jiu-jitsu, everything in life. I have to be prepared for any kind of change. I always wanted to be ready for a competition, a meeting, to meet with my team and motivate them to reach their goals. Because I believe when you're prepared you may not have an answer for everything but you can explain your vision better. And when you make people understand your vision and they want to join your vision, they join fully aware and carrying your vision with you, so the chances of you achieving your goals are much higher."

Leo has dedicated himself to a sport and most sports involve competition. I went back to Leo's jiu-jitsu competition experience and asked him if there were any rituals he followed to mentally prepare for a competition. He answered, "I keep learning that it's really important to be mentally prepared. I started reading about mental preparation. I do some meditation and self-talk. The day of competition I'm just in my mind telling myself that I'm ready, that I'm good, that I'm strong, that I'm fast, that I'm ready for the challenge whatever or whoever comes my way. Competition is different from daily training. Bad self-talk in competition can ruin everything, and it happened before; I looked at a guy and said to myself, 'Oh he's bigger and looks stronger,' and BOOM, the match is over right there! So I believe that positive self-talk, meditation and the ability to stay calm when things don't start the way I want are important. I like to set the pace but if things don't go my way I have to be prepared to say to myself, 'Ok, it's not the end of the world' and realize I still have time to work. Meditation helps me to keep things clear even when things don't go my way. I try to meditate at least once a week, and when it comes closer to the competition I try to do it every day the whole week before the competition, especially if it's a big competition.

Leo went on to explain the difference in competing in small competitions versus larger competitions. He said, "I use the smaller competitions, such as the IBJJF Opens, as just preparation. It's a way to test what I've been doing in training and try new things, to sharpen up my technique for Worlds or Pan Ams (which are more prestigious competitions). I take more chances in the small competitions because I want to see if the techniques I've been working on during training is going to work in competition."

For the next question, I wanted to see how Leo dealt with failure. I stated, "In business as in fighting, setbacks can feel extremely personal. You lose a fight, and that is really personal, especially if you feel you didn't fight to your full potential. In business, you may lose a client or a deal, you may lose employees, several things can go wrong. How do you deal with setbacks?" Leo replied, "One of the books I read was about mental preparation, and there was an exercise in it. I feel stronger now psychologically than when I was in the business world before, I used to deal pretty bad with setbacks. I used to feel like I was letting myself down, or my family or my friends. But now what I do is I give myself 10 minutes to vent, be mad, complain, and make excuses or whatever. Then after that 10 minutes it's done, let's move forward. I don't allow self-doubt after that 10 minutes. During the 10 minutes I can say whatever I want to myself including the worst things I could tell myself (laughs), but after 10 minutes 'All right, okay, that already happened. What am I going to do next so that doesn't happen again?' It's not easy of course, it's hard, especially in the beginning, but it's been working very well.[1] And the other thing I learned is nobody gives a shit if you win or lose. People that actually care for you, you're still their hero. We usually are worried about how people will look at us after we fail, but the people that really matter, they don't care. They want the best for you so they know that one failure doesn't define you."

I told Leo how much I appreciated what he just said because it ties back to the positive self-talk, even when you fail. Self-talk is even more important when you experience failure because it's what will carry you on to the next step and moving forward. Leo agreed by explaining the self-talk he may have with himself if he experiences temporary failure: "It's nothing, you did it before, it's not the first time you've lost, let's pick it up and let's keep going." These statements help him move forward with purpose and a commitment to improve.

The last question I had for Leo was "How do you measure success?" Leo thought hard and slowly answered, "That's a really good question, I'm not really good at measuring success. I feel that I won't be able to measure if I succeeded until I die. Of course, you can measure accomplishments, but for me success is a much broader thing. It's about happiness, it's about life, it's about family, it's about everything, and so I feel that I need more time to be able to measure if I've succeeded or not (laughs). If I was a good husband, if I was a good son, if I was a good parent, it's about much more. I can definitely measure accomplishments, like I wanted to be a world champion and I am a world champion so I accomplished that, and that is an unbelievable feeling. But, it's not success. It's just weird, because as soon as you step off the podium you're already asking yourself 'What's next?' So all these things are temporary; success to me is a much bigger thing. Success is about how many lives you impacted for good; it's about everything, so I just feel I need more time to evaluate that."

There are many accomplishments, including BJJ championships that Leo continues to achieve on his own. Leo trained at and was a BJJ Instructor at Soul fighters Brazilian Jiu-Jitsu Association, CT, where I met him. He now is the owner and lead instructor at American Martial Art Academy in Mississippi. He trains, teaches, travels, and competes regularly. He is living the life he chooses, and I truly believe he is enjoying every minute of it. That in and of itself is his biggest accomplishment. Leo is following his dream of being a multiple time world champion and I believe he will accomplish that and more. The journey he is on does not have an end.

I went on to say to Leo "with all the goals you've accomplished and will continue to accomplish, your success is almost guaranteed." Leo has been a positive influence on my life in the few years I've known him, and he continues to lead and inspire. Leo thanked me, and we ended the meeting with an "Oss" (I'm not exactly sure what "Oss" means or where it comes from, but in Brazilian Jiu-Jitsu "Oss" is a greeting, a farewell, an affirmation, and a sign of respect all in one).

Leo is a true martial artist in the sense of striving for perfection. He is constantly challenging himself by competing in BJJ tournaments. His biggest competitor is himself and he is always looking to do better than he did in the previous tournament. BJJ competition is his classroom where he expresses himself freely and he is learning about himself, sharpening his attributes and reducing his limitations. In the world of business BJJ competition could be likened to a boardroom meeting or a sales call where the preparation and hard work finally pays off, and if it doesn't it doesn't mean the end of the world, just that something needs to be fine-tuned for the next time. Leo has adopted the motto "0 talent, 100% hard work." Leo relies on his hard work, not his natural ability. He feels that hard work trumps everything else. If we honestly look at our performance in a boardroom meeting, a sales call, or an interview, we can see what we did well and what needs work. As in martial arts the work is constant, because if you're not working someone else is, and it may be your next competitor.

Stay Determined – Key Points:

- Walk your own path. Decide what you want for yourself and pursue it with the passion it deserves. Outside influences want what they want for you. You are responsible for your own happiness.
- Compete with yourself, all the time. Challenge yourself to be better than you were in the last competition, meeting, negotiation, sales call, or interview.
- Break down your goals into smaller goals. Smaller goals help you achieve the big goals. Smaller goals can change, big goals usually stay the same.
- Being prepared helps you increase your chances of achieving your goals.
- Watch what you say (to yourself). Self-talk is powerful and should be guarded. Use positive self-talk especially when things go wrong, it is the best way to turn things around in your favor.
- Failure doesn't define you. Learn to move on from setbacks quickly. Give yourself time to vent if needed, but be quick about it. Move on with purpose.
- Success is personal. You may have a vision of success that is totally different from someone else's and that is okay. Keep striving for your own version of success.

Chapter 5: Overcome Adversity

Jared Gordon is an MMA fighter with an amazing story. His current record as a professional Mixed Martial Artist is an impressive 14 wins and 2 losses. He is currently in the UFC lightweight division and in Jared's own words "that's where I will retire." He was the Cage Fury Fighting Championships (CFFC) Featherweight Champion and the Duelo De Gigantes MMA Lightweight Champion.

I was introduced to Jared by my friend, Mike Jaramillo, a BJJ Black Belt under Renzo Gracie and MMA grappling coach to several up and coming MMA fighters. Mike briefly gave me a rundown of Jared's history and referred me to the mma.com article titled "The Unbreakable Man" by Shaun Al-Shatti (Shaun Al-Shatti has also written another article on Jared Gordon titled "Still Unbroken: Jared Gordon's Harrowing Road to UFC 211). I immediately liked Jared, not having met him yet, after I read that article so fittingly titled "The Unbreakable Man." In a nutshell, the article portrays Jared as a drug addict who fights every day to beat his addiction (I also deal with demons daily. They may or may not be addiction but I definitely have issues to contend with.) For Jared, the drugs have included heroin, opiates and cocaine, and his addiction has led him to jail, rehab, being homeless, and multiple overdoses that almost claimed his life. Jared is an extremist in every way which has been his blessing and his curse. On one hand, he struggles with his addiction to some of the harshest chemicals known to man, and on the other hand Jared is fighting to become champion in one of the most extreme sports on the planet, Mixed Martial Arts. Mind you, he also is competing on the biggest stage in Mixed Martial Arts, the UFC. It is an incredible story of perseverance and grit. If anyone has the mental toughness to overcome adversity and still be successful, it's Jared. My interview with Jared focused on the mental toughness required to overcome the type of adversity Jared has overcome. I thought if only we could catch a glimpse of the perseverance Jared encompasses, maybe we could use this insight for our own struggles. Jared is constantly overcoming obstacles and challenges as we all are, therefore, I felt extremely fortunate to learn about Jared's fight mentality. What I identify with the most about anyone who's successful is the ability to get back up after being knocked down. We all love a winner, and so do I, but what I love even more is the winner who comes back time after time, setback after setback, and still finds a way to win when it counts. Jared is that type of winner.

My first question for Jared was with regards to his fights in the Duelo De Gigantes MMA series held in Mexico. It was an ultimate fighter style tournament where a fighter keeps advancing after each win until he gets to the championship. Jared won all four of his fights in that series and thus the championship. Jared received a belt and an oversized $100,000 check. However, the actual prize money was never sent his way. In the mma.com article "The Unbreakable Man" I had read that Jared considered it sort of a blessing that he never received that prize money. I found that statement very intriguing so I asked Jared to explain his thoughts on not receiving that prize money. He answered, "I was obviously upset that I didn't get the prize money. I fought four fights, and I won the whole tournament and they never paid me but at the time I was in a certain place in my life where if I had received $100,000 it probably would have been a bad thing. Who knows what I would have went and done...I had a terrible drug addiction, even though I was sober when I fought that fight (Duelo De Gigantes Championship), after that fight I had a shoulder surgery and I relapsed because I was taking the pain pills (for the recovery from surgery), and I went back to doing heroin. That was two or three months after I won the fight (the surgery), so I still would have had a good amount of money, hopefully I would have (laughs), so who knows what I would have went and done at that point." In speaking with Jared and learning about him I noticed he has an ability to see things from different perspectives, a trait that has enabled him to rise from hitting rock bottom and use his experiences to his advantage. He is constantly looking forward, and he only looks back as a guide to move him in the right direction. His outlook makes it seem as if the pain and anguish he has experienced was meant to be. It was all with a purpose, and he finds that purpose in every experience. It is a remarkable ability and something that we all can learn from. The ability to learn from our mistakes, trials, and tribulations is no new concept by any means, yet we rarely see it being utilized in real life. Jared is utilizing that ability, and he is a rising star in the UFC because of it.

During the interview, I learned that Jared started fighting 13 years ago, he started his amateur career when he was 17 years old. (I learned the day of this interview that Jared would be receiving a surprise 30th birthday party that evening.) He started with boxing then jiu-jitsu, then he picked up kickboxing. Within four months of training, he had his first amateur MMA fight.

I asked Jared for a snapshot of his MMA fight career

path. Jared stated, "I started fighting amateur at 17, I remember thinking I'm just going to do it as a bucket list item and cross it off my bucket list saying I fought an amateur MMA fight...so I fought, and I fell in love. I fell in love with Martial Arts. So I had another fight and I won. Then I had another fight and I fought this kid and we were both 3-0 at the time, we fought for the Newbreed 147-pound championship. We had a trilogy, I was winning the first fight, but I got cut, and I lost; they stopped the fight. Then we had a rematch; I won by split decision. Then we had another fight for the trilogy; and I crushed him in the third fight. Then I went on to have four more fights as an amateur; I won another title. Then I had my pro debut in 2011. I went pro for CFFC, and I won. Throughout all this time, there were lots of ups and downs. I was in and out of rehab for my addiction. There were lots of ups and downs. But I went on, I kept fighting-fighting-fighting! (Jared rotates his hand in a forward circular motion to emphasize the continuity). I was 9-0 (as a pro). I fought for the CFFC championship, I actually lost that fight...I was winning, I was crushing the fight then I got hurt, and they stopped the fight on me; the doctor stopped the fight due to my eye being pretty bad. They gave me a rematch for the title, which I won. Then I won two or three more fights and I got signed to the UFC, in the Dana White 'Looking for a Fight' show."

I asked Jared to explain the details of getting signed to the UFC through the UFC show. He explained, "They were coming to see my fight and I had to put on a show and win impressively and that's what I did, I went out there whipped some ass and they signed me (smiles). I won my first two UFC fights and unfortunately I lost my last one but I'll rebound and that's all I can do."

With Jared's ability to overcome adversity, I wanted to

really understand how he perceived adversity, because I believed it is his perception of adversity that allowed him to handle it so well. So I asked Jared an open ended question about how he views adversity. Jared answered, "When I look back at it, I'm happy that I can say I've overcome it...and that it makes you a stronger person and you grow from adversity, and that you need adversity to become successful...but then when it happens to me, when I'm dealing with new adversity it's like the worst thing in the world. Right now, I'm dealing with some new adversity, I moved to Milwaukee, I'm training with a new team, I'm coming off this loss from my last fight, this is adversity, I have to bounce back, I have to win my next fight. Obviously, you have to win every fight, but this is an important fight for me. You know, even though it looks like I'm doing fairly well, I'm 2 and 1 in the UFC, so it's not like I'm doing horrible, but you don't want to lose two in a row...you have fears and doubts. If you're a business owner it's the same thing, you open a business or you want to start a business and adversity comes...for me, if I feel like it's good for me but I'm scared to do it, then I know that I have to do it. Where I see a lot of (other) people, if they think they should do something and they're scared to do it, and then they don't do it. And then later on in life they probably have like a mid-life crisis or something like that because they didn't make the jump (chuckles). So I'm an extremist; I think that's why I became a drug addict as well. For me, I go big or go home. There's no in between. I'm not going to do anything mediocre. If I'm going to do drugs well I'm going to shoot drugs, I'm not going to (just) smoke weed, I'm going to shoot heroin and shoot cocaine...and (conversely) if I want to be an MMA fighter, well I want to fight in the UFC and become champion. I guess that could be good and bad where I take things to an extreme, and it could be a negative thing or it could be a positive thing, but now I'm trying to make it all a positive thing."

I could tell that Jared was passionate about what he was saying based off the tempo and energy in his voice. He spoke at a crisp New York pace, and his confidence inferred a "take it or leave it" attitude. Jared said something that really resonated with me when he said, "If I feel like something's good for me but I'm scared to do it, then I know I have to do it." I was impressed by the insight he provided because I can think of times when I wanted to do something but I was scared for whatever reason, usually the fear is of what others may think. You may have experienced the same thing, the urge to say something in a business meeting, or to ask for the business in a sales encounter, or to ask for a promotion, or to start a business, and you may not have acted on it. If we're honest with ourselves, it's usually the fear of what others may think that holds us back. Speaking with Jared encouraged me to face that fear and realize, like Jared does, that I have to do it. The times that I have faced that fear and conquered my anxiety over what others may think, those times are the most liberating moments I can remember. In speaking with Jared, I felt he armed me with more confidence to create more of those moments in my life, and my hope is that you as a reader of this book, and a student of life, are inspired to do the same thing.

I wanted the conversation with Jared to go even deeper into how he overcomes adversity, so I asked him, "What has been your biggest setback professionally and what did you learn from it that's helping you now?" Jared pondered the question then responded, "I've made a lot of small mistakes in my career. I missed weight in my first UFC fight. I lost my last UFC fight. For me, it's a setback; people would say 'It's part of the game; everyone loses.' I think there's only two guys that haven't lost, Jon Jones and Khabib, and Jon Jones is on steroids. Khabib is the only guy who's undefeated (currently). George St. Pierre, they call him the GOAT (Greatest Of All Time) and he's lost twice, he got knocked out by Matt Serra, and he lost to Matt Hughes. Everyone has a setback in life; for me it's myself. My biggest setback is when I get in my own way. There's times when I didn't make the jump when I should've made the jump...so I think the man in the mirror is my biggest setback, if I let it be. I don't want to say that when I failed at fighting, or failed career wise, it was a setback. I would call them more or less just learning experiences, yes they're setbacks, but for me I needed these things to happen...my rock bottoms have all been self-induced. It was because of me it wasn't anyone else...I did it to myself."

I asked Jared what his process was with dealing with these negative experiences he referred to as rock bottoms. He explained, "Every time I've had something bad happen to me and I look back at it, it always seems to bring something else into the light. When things are happening to me, I'm like 'Why is this happening?' then a couple of months go by and I can see 'I needed this to happen to grow.' And there's rhyme and reason to where I look back and I can see why things happen. It made me turn into a better person, it was for a positive (result) in the end."

When looking back on his experiences, especially the negative experiences, Jared had processed the experiences to look for what could be learned from them. In doing so, he not only eliminated regret, one of the most destructive feelings, but he also empowered himself by really learning from his mistakes and even saying, "I needed this to happen to grow." This is a powerful statement when applied with consistency and belief and it has led Jared to where he is today, an elite athlete in the UFC. Think of what this statement could do for you. What past experiences are still holding you back with feelings of regret? What if you said to yourself "I needed this to happen to grow," would things move forward for you in a new and more positive direction? Of course they would. Try using this statement and see for yourself how it can give you the perspective you need in order to take a bad experience and improve from it.

Jared went on to detail his process for dealing with new challenges, "When I go to jump at things, I do it only if it feels true in my heart. If I really feel I have to do something then I'll do it. My last big thing is I moved to Milwaukee to train with a new team. I was going through some things...I was coming off my loss and there were some personal things happening, and literally all at one moment, I had an epiphany, where I was like, 'I have to move.' It wasn't something over time that I thought about, it literally just hit me and I was like 'I've got to go.' It was like 11:30 at night, and I was sitting on my couch in my living room, everyone was sleeping, my parents were upstairs and for some reason my Mom came down the steps (Jared explains how his Mom has a heightened sense of intuition), and she asked me 'Are you all right?' I said 'yes, why?' and she said 'I don't know I just had this weird feeling.' And I'm sitting there thinking to myself 'I've got to get out of New York, I've got to move.' I tell her 'yeah I'm fine but I've got to leave.' She said, 'what are you talking about?' I explained to her my feelings and she said 'alright, you've got to do what you've got to do.' And within twenty minutes, I made that decision like 'I'm getting out of here' and so far it's been the right choice." Jared explains that he has had other epiphanies but this was the clearest one he's had thus far.

"This was a big move for me. I've been successful with my team and coaches so I didn't leave because of the team or coaches. I had some personal things going on but the coaching was great, I was just missing some things that I needed, certain tweaks. Going away to a new gym and new place there are obviously cons as well, but the positives outweighed the cons."

I asked Jared a question regarding his ability and skill level. I asked him what skill he feels helps him the most in a fight. He thought hard about it and responded, "I think physically my cardio and my ground and pound (ground and pound is a term used for a fighting style where a fighter takes the opponent down to the ground and beats them into submission with his/her fists) are my bread and butter. I know I have good striking too." Then Jared reframed the question and focused on what he thought was his biggest asset, his mind. Jared said, "Mentally, my will and my desire to win and to come out on top, I have to come out on top! The only time I'm going to lose is if the ref jumps in and stops it or the doctor stops it on me; that's the only time that I've lost. My one loss in the UFC, I broke five bones in my face, my orbital floor was blown out, my eye was completely shut, I was bleeding like a gut fish, and the doctor came in between the third and the fourth round and said, 'We're calling it, your eye is so bad…' I actually almost lost my eye in that fight, and I was begging them 'Please let me fight.'…The doctor said, 'You're insane, we're not letting you fight.' My last fight (the only other loss) I got hit with a punch, and I hit the floor and I hopped up and there was an exchange, then I got caught in a bad position where the ref thought I wasn't intelligently defending myself and he stopped the fight. I sat up and said to the ref, 'C'mon bro, I wasn't knocked out, yeah I got dropped, but I wasn't unconscious or anything.' So the only time I'm going to lose is if I go out on my shield. It's (most likely) not going to be a decision fight, it's going to be a war no matter what. So I think my will and my desire to break people, if it's a fight of attrition, I'm always going to come out on top… 'Who wants it more, who's going to dig deeper?' I think that's a huge part of my skillset."

I asked Jared how he developed his will to win and he answered, "I think throughout all my experiences in life, going through all the adversity, I just want to be successful. I need to be successful. My style of fighting is that I'm a pressure fighter so it goes hand in hand, I keep coming forward…I don't want to stop, I'm not moving backwards. If you hit me I'm not going to start running away from you. I think my lifestyle, my life experiences, and the way I fight are the same thing, it's just go! Go, Go, Go!"

I clearly saw the connection with his extreme mindset and his style of fighting and commended Jared for using this mindset in a setting that is productive and has benefited him so well, in the UFC octagon. We all have adversity and challenges, how can we use them to fuel us? Maybe it's as simple as just seeing that if we are still here, alive and breathing, that means that we have a purpose, and we must fulfill it by being the best version of ourselves in any endeavor. If you are reading this book it is highly probable that you want to be successful. Being able to find your will to succeed when you have every reason to give up, that's what determines your progress. We go through our challenges for various reasons, it's up to us to see those challenges as a reason to grow and then embrace the opportunities in front of us, and like Jared, just go!

I then asked Jared, "What advice would you give to somebody who wants to develop that attribute, the will to win?" Jared said, "You have to have a burning desire to be successful. It doesn't have to be in the cage. If you want something you have to do whatever you can, fight tooth and nail to get it. You'll know, for example in the ring, you'll know if you really want to do this. When you have certain experiences, for instance when my eye was hanging out of my head and I still wanted to fight. That's a point in your life where you'll ask yourself 'do I really want to do this or not?' I sat in the hospital for seven days after that in the head trauma unit. I speak to other professional fighters that told me that they would've quit after that, if they got that hurt they would've stopped fighting. That was NEVER an option in my head. I went to the hospital and I got the X-Ray and the doctor told me that I might be blind. I said 'No I'm not, I'm not fucking blind, are you crazy?' And he said, 'This is probably your last fight ever.' And I said 'no it's not.' I go to the hospital sometimes and the doctor's like 'Maybe you should find a new career,' and I'm like 'Maybe you should shut the fuck up (chuckles)'...you're not going to stop me from wanting to complete my goal...It's going to come to a point where you're in a position where you have to make a choice 'Do I want to keep going or is this not really for me?' So you'll know when you're there I think."

I then asked Jared if you get to the breaking point where you either want to keep going or you don't, and you decide yes I want to keep going, will you find a reserve you didn't know you had? Jared replied, "You're going to dig, and you're going to find it. Your body will break before your mind breaks. So far that's what's happened to me in my fights. My eye broke, but I didn't want to stop...It wasn't up to me anymore, it was up to the doctor. I commented that if it was up to Jared, he probably would've kept going. He said, "Yeah, I would've fucking fought man!" I then said, "And you would've probably won." Jared then said, "I was up on all the judge's scorecards...but it was out of my hands." I said to Jared, "I think that if you hit that breaking point and you say 'Fuck it, I'm gonna keep going,' then your body will cooperate." Jared agreed "Yeah, it goes on autopilot."

My next question for Jared was a fun question, "If you could fight anybody who would it be and why?" Jared answered, "I would love to fight Khabib (he's referring to Khabib Nurmagomedov, the current UFC lightweight champion), because we have the same style. The game that Mike (Jaramillo) has showed me, he showed me everything on the ground, and if it wasn't for Mike I wouldn't be where I am. It's the same game." Mike Jaramillo is a BJJ black belt and Jared's grappling coach. I refer to Mike's style of grappling as a pressure style where he gives his opponent no space to move maintaining dominant position, then going for a submission. "I don't think he's fought anybody that understands it the way that I understand it. It's the same exact game. My roommate back in Milwaukee, we train a "shit ton" together, and he recently rolled (grappled) with Khabib. He said it was the same (as with me)...identical feel. He's (Khabib is) obviously a massive competitor and probably one of the best fighters ever, but I think I am too. Win or lose I would love to fight him."

My last question was "What's your next big goal?" Jared immediately replied, "For me right now the next goal is to win my next fight. I have no option but to win this next fight. And I will. And then move on from there."

During this interview I really felt the belief that Jared has in himself. He has overcome so much adversity and uses every obstacle as fuel to accomplish bigger and better things. In my humble opinion, Jared is no doubt championship material. Whatever challenges he has had, he has reframed the experience, and they are now stepping stones. I can't help but think that without these stepping stones, how else can one climb to the top? One thing I know about Jared is that he will continue to climb, one step at a time.

Overcome Adversity – Key Points:

- Look for the good, even when it sucks. Not every experience is going to be a good one, however, we can still take something good from every experience. Finding a purpose in every experience is a matter of perspective.
- Keep moving toward your goals relentlessly. Life has ups and downs, not all paths are a straight line, simply keep progressing in spite of the bumps in the road. Steady progress builds exponentially over time.
- Be ready for your opportunity. Opportunities may come unexpectedly. You can be ready by staying prepared with consistent training.
- If you know you need to do something, but you are scared to do it, then run towards it. This is the best way to overcome your fear and reach your goals.
- Setbacks are learning experiences. You need them in order to improve. When you encounter a setback use the statement "I needed this to happen to grow," and it will change your perspective.
- Draw from the pain you've experienced, especially the hardships and stumbling blocks during your journey towards your goals. This pain will push you when it counts the most, when you want to win more than the other person.
- If the desire to win is inside you, keep digging, and keep putting yourself in positions to attain your goals, no matter how uncomfortable they may be. This is how you will find your true desire.

Chapter 6: Learn from your Experience

I have had the opportunity to meet many extraordinary people in my own Martial Arts journey. One of my initial introductions to the sense of community amongst Brazilian Jiu-Jitsu practitioners was when my dad introduced me to his friend and business associate at the time, Mike Jaramillo, a BJJ black belt under Renzo Gracie and John Danaher. That introduction was a decade ago when I started my BJJ journey. I clearly remember how Mike was so excited to speak with me. Now I get it – the kinship felt amongst BJJ practitioners is universal as it is a lifestyle that changes people for the better. I remember Mike's first question for me when we first spoke on the phone: "So have you fallen in love with it yet?" Mike knows it doesn't take long to get bit by the BJJ love bug. My answer was a resounding "Yes!" Soon after that conversation, Mike went on to compete in the IBJJF European Championships and win his black belt division. I continue to be impressed by Mike, as he is still competing and challenging himself on and off the mats. Just before this interview, I had rolled (live sparring in Brazilian Jiu-Jitsu) with Mike. He invited me to train at Bronx Martial Arts Academy, a Renzo Gracie affiliate. The academy is run by Professor Doug Pelinkovic, a formidable martial artist, consummate professional, and Mike's business partner. Mike usually trains at Doug's academy on Saturday mornings and this is where I met Mike to train and interview him. I can personally attest to Mike's experience and high level on the mats. I got the chance to witness his grappling prowess when I trained with him. When it comes to grappling, Mike is an absolute beast!

Mike is a 3rd degree Brazilian Jiu-Jitsu black belt under the world renowned Master Renzo Gracie and Professor John Danaher. Mike is an IBJJF European Champion, and IBJJF No-Gi World Champion. His love for grappling has led him to be a first-class MMA grappling coach for athletes competing in the UFC, Bellator, World Series of Fighting, Cage Fury Fighting Championships, and the Professional Fighter's League. Mike is not only a student of the art, he is a teacher, and like most good teachers he is generous with his knowledge and willing to help others learn and grow. In fact, Mike introduced me to Jared Gordon and helped me secure that interview. Mike was Jared's grappling coach and can be seen as a corner man in the footage of several of Jared's MMA fights. Mike helped me in the upcoming interview by providing an understanding of how Martial Arts has helped him in business, as well as what attributes he looks to cultivate in himself and the fighters he coaches.

Mike is an accomplished entrepreneur, owning several businesses previously and currently. I wanted to get a good understanding of how Mike has used Martial Arts to help him on his Entrepreneurial path, and vice versa. I began the interview with Mike by first asking him to explain his entrepreneurial experience. Mike began, "I own an electrical company which has about fifty people in it. I've had that company for about fifteen years right now so I was probably in my mid-thirties when I started that. I've also had quite a few other business. I owned four health clubs which I built from the ground up. The guys that I have (in the electrical company) are multi-taskers. I've taken people that didn't know electrical, but I've seen something in them such as hard work with detail orientation, and I've taught them electrical. I've taken them from other trades, whether they were carpenters or concrete guys, and I've lured them over to the electrical. Being that I had these multi-taskers, I got into building (literally constructing) businesses from the ground up. So I've built four health clubs, about 15,000 square feet, with saunas, spin rooms, boxing rooms, yoga rooms, steam rooms, full fledge health clubs. I bought and sold them, and I still have one (that I own). In the gym business at one time, memberships were running about $100 monthly. That has changed. The gym business has become saturated, unless you have a large number of health clubs the business has gotten very tight. You can't have one or two and be an absentee owner. It's tough to make money at them. On all of them I've had Doug Pelinkovic as my partner (Doug Pelinkovic is a Black Belt in Brazilian Jiu-Jitsu, as well as a 3rd degree Black Belt in Shotokan Karate, and also a successful business owner). I've also gone into other business. I had a full fledge restaurant, I did a Latin Fusion place. These are all learning experiences. I've had so many failures and I wouldn't trade any of them. Because of those failures I feel like I went to the Harvard School of Business. I've always tried to walk away and learn my lesson, whether good or bad. So I've had a Latin Fusion restaurant that was successful for a period but I didn't like that business. The restaurant business is quite hard especially for someone coming in as a rookie so I made quite a few mistakes. I thought because I like to go out to eat a lot that I would know the restaurant business, and that's as far from it as possible (chuckles). I also at one point owned a bakery, more because I was dating a girl that really loved to bake. I used the same principle, I've always been lucky enough to have a vision of seeing a product at its end stage. I had an idea of what I wanted this bakery to look like and we built a bakery. Also a very good business, it was a small bakery. When that relationship ended I got out of that. I did another restaurant type business, a healthy eatery. Both the bakery and the healthy eatery still exist, I sold them after three or four years.

I still continue with the electrical business, and as I've gotten older, I'm a year away from turning fifty, the drive to do more and more businesses isn't there; it's learning to be more detailed in the businesses that I have. There's a Japanese saying which I think applies to many things in business: 'Instead of making many holes make one hole, but make that hole super deep'...so my philosophy has changed quite a bit. I am very driven in the electrical business now, along with Jiu-Jitsu. When I had multiple business along with the electrical business, the electrical business consisted of 10 to 15 people. Now that's not the case; the electrical business employs 50 people, so I'm really driven in that business. My main focus is the client. I feel that the client deserves to have a complete product that's giving back to them, and the client gets catered to at a different level. Most contractors don't approach their service from a business aspect, because they're typically not business people. They're contractors that went into business. I've learned to become a business man through failures and life lessons. I've been lucky enough to fail many times (chuckles). Each time I've asked myself, 'Why did I fail and how can I change that?' Then I apply the correction the next time."

Mike described how service is at the very core of his business and has always been his main goal "Sometimes people will say to me 'I want to be my own boss.' I say

'There's no such thing.' In every business there is a client or a customer that buys your product, you work for that person, understand that. I've understood that. Whatever it may be, if you own a hardware store and a customer comes in to buy a set of pliers, you greet them, you thank them, and you show them all the options and explain them. That's the type of service that gets you the repeat customer. Now that guy will go out of his way to tell a friend about you. I've taken that concept of service and applied it to my business and it has been amazing for me. Now I say 'no' to more jobs than I accept. I pick and choose the jobs I want. I'm not saying this to be cocky in any way, I'm trying to get business people to understand that if you apply the concept of service to any business it will help you be successful. Be thankful, and go above and beyond to service your customers, and build your business one customer at a time."

As I found out just how much business experience Mike had, I was very impressed with the magnitude of his business background. I thought more of the interview would be to gain his insight as a Martial Artist and coach of several MMA fighters. However, the business aspect of the interview played a larger role because I then began to correlate how business and martial arts have both played equally important roles in Mike's life. I am impressed with his business background and am glad he shared it. I am especially impressed with the statement he made with regards to being grateful for his failures. In Martial Arts and in Life, I realize that embracing failure and learning from it is what determines a person's success and how far they take their art or profession.

I asked Mike how long he has been practicing martial arts. He responded, "I started in 1998 with Shotokan Karate. At that Shotokan Karate dojo, they started a Ne-

Waza class, which means ground fighting in Japanese. A gentleman who had been training in Japan had come over to the United States. They asked me to participate in a class because they were looking for students, and that's the first step in how I found Brazilian Jiu-Jitsu. That gentleman competed in an event, and I went to the event, and I saw these guys wearing Renzo Gracie shirts. I didn't know who they were but they were winning all their matches which intrigued me to find out who Renzo Gracie was. That's how I ended up, 20 years later, still being part of that (Renzo Gracie) family."

Going back to his business background, I asked Mike how long he had been an entrepreneur. Mike thought about it and answered "At the age of 18, my neighbor's father was an electrician, and I used to work for him in the summertime. His wife had terminal leukemia, and he was thinking about getting out of the business. When his wife passed, he decided to go on a road trip and get out of the business. So the two of us (his son and myself) spoke, and we decided to do small electrical jobs, and we formed a company. His father lent us $12,500 in 1987 so that we could buy a truck and some tools. That's how we got started. So at the age of 18 I was a business owner. That went for about thirteen years. In the year 2000 when the economy first crashed, things got really tight. We lost some large clients and we weren't making any money. That puts pressure on partners, we both had families, and he decided to go on his own. He actually wanted to take the business over and force me out. At that time, I was not the guy that dealt with the client, I dealt with the jobs, so he felt he could get rid of me. We had three major clients, and he held on to most of the work, while I held on to one client. I was doing work for the school construction authority. It was 2001, and I attempted to go full force into running a gym, hoping that I would walk away from the electrical. Unfortunately, it didn't start out like that. The gym just started and wasn't making money. I had a mortgage, and a family, so I had to go back to the construction. I got an opportunity to return to the school construction authority with one small school job, and I did it myself with one helper. At the very end of the job, they wanted to meet me. They were so impressed with the work that they offered me a second job. That grew to more jobs and I hired more help. Some of the project managers from the school construction authority left and found new companies, and they would call me to do work for them because they knew my work. That was the start of me growing an electrical business by myself. During that time I was also doing other things, some of them resulted in the failures I spoke about earlier, and now I focus on the electrical business and the gym."

Mike has tried many businesses and not all of them have succeeded however his persistence in entrepreneurship has allowed him to establish a profitable electrical company with a solid reputation, and a gym that continues to grow. Mike is a life learner and his martial arts background helps him in that aspect, he is always learning and improving. Mike considers his failures his best teachers and a blessing because they have helped him grow. In martial arts if you are not failing you are not trying hard enough. In life that is also the case, especially in business. If you get complacent and play it safe, you may get by for a while, but sooner or later you will become irrelevant. You must push the pace and look for new opportunities as a business owner because the only constant is change. Therefore you must be willing to change, all the time.

My next question for Mike was about his coaching style as an MMA coach. I wanted to know what qualities Mike instills in his fighters, and why? Mike's explanation went as follows "There's different fighters so you have to look at the individual and determine what they need to improve on. Some fighters maybe have taken fighting up later in life. That person may have an issue where he's never learned the urgency of having to produce under extreme pressure such as getting out of a bad spot or attacking when there's little time left on the clock. He's never learned to dig deep while having to overcome adversity and have no quit. So what they'll do is go to a safe zone. For example let's say in an MMA fight, a guy passes a guard, he goes to side control and he *pins*! Because he feels that's safe. But I don't need safe, I need success. I need him to transfer to the next positive point, that could be a strike, that could be an elbow, or some form of a wedge where he can manipulate the angle to hit. So with that type of fighter I need to figure out how to change that man's mindset. It's not that different from business, because what you're doing is forming a new habit. In business maybe it's the habit of waking up at 5 o'clock in the morning every single day and getting on your computer and doing your work. There's no difference in the fighter. I need to create a new habit in him, so when adversity happens, 'Man I need you to dig deep, so deep in you, that right now you're going to stand up and fight harder than you've ever fought before in your life.' I'll simulate time restrictions while training with fighters to try and change them.

"If you take a kid that's been a good wrestler from the ages of 5 through 10 and has wrestled in leagues and competed, he's already been molded from an early age to have no quit in him. He may not win the national championship, but if you wrestle that guy he doesn't know how to stop. He doesn't know how to quit. He keeps coming, and coming, and coming! It's been instilled so deep in him. You'll see a lot of high level businessmen that were very accomplished wrestlers because they were taught at an early age to keep driving and driving! They don't know how to give up. So if a person hasn't done that from an early age or maybe they started fighting later on, they don't have the same advantage. Even if they've been competitive in something like soccer, it's different. Soccer is a team sport. And if we're equating sports to business, if you own your own business, that's just you. In fighting, it's just you. You can hide in a team setting. You can do great things as a team, but you have the crutch of the others. In fighting, there's no crutch, you're there, it's all you. So I need to change the mindset of the fighters that start later in life. Sometimes you can't. Sometimes they get scared and they run, but they need to self-evaluate and be honest. I have constant conversations with my fighters about mindset. I require them to be detailed and do the homework on their opponents and also themselves. I tell them that they have to look at themselves and ask themselves if they're putting in the effort. I don't want to see them talk about what they are going to do. I want to see the work ethic. Everything will fall into place with work ethic. All those dreams are just dreams without work ethic. It's like a businessman saying 'I want to be rich.' What does that mean? If you want to make money that will come as a by-product of being detailed, having a tremendous work ethic, caring, and putting the time in. There are all these boxes that need to be checked and then you'll see this money if that's what you want. If you want a successful business, all these boxes have to be checked first. If you want to be champion all these boxes have to be checked first. I need every box to be checked."

Since this interview took place I have had time to reflect about the correlation Mike made between fighters and business people. He stated that running a business is more like an individual sport than a team sport. I have gone back and forth in my mind with that because I am also aware of the mindset that a running a business is more like running a team than an individual activity. After some reflecting and contemplating I understand and can validate what Mike was saying. In the event that things work out, the team should get credit, and a good leader will make sure that happens. However, if things don't work out, the leader/business owner is accountable, there's no one else, it falls on the leader. That's the cost of doing business. In that aspect it's just like fighting.

Mike explained how he feels journaling is so important and a requirement for his fighters. Mike says "I tell my fighters to ask themselves, 'Am I putting my work in, am I waking up early, am I taking notes and keeping a journal?' I need them to keep a journal. I need them writing in their journal every day, and I need them to re-read their journal. The written word is tremendous. It engrains things at a deeper level in the subconscious. So I make it a requirement for my fighters. This really equates to business as well. Whether you want to start a business, be more successful in your current business, or if you work for someone, it doesn't matter, you must take the time to keep notes and keep a 'to do list' for the next day. The mind is so scattered, and there are all these boxes that need to be checked so we need that journal as a back up to help us focus. I require my fighters to be detailed, meaning they must break down what went well and what went wrong during their training. Then they can write down the next steps to improve their technical errors. Then they can go back to the journal and check on their progress, making sure they have addressed their errors. We have to see this progress so we have to write it down. This can go for business, say you have a meeting with a client and you didn't land the account. If you took notes, now you can reread your notes and come up with a plan to land the account at the next meeting. These are the same types of strategies I use with the fighters to improve their performance. We have a lot of conversations about the psychological aspect of the game and that includes being detailed, taking notes, and keeping a journal."

I asked Mike if he felt the mental training he works on with his fighters was something he emphasized even more than the physical training. Mike said, "The physical for most fighters at the high level is a given. Because it's something that they enjoy. They enjoy lifting weights, they enjoy scrapping on the ground, they like running. For the average person they may not enjoy exercising, but for the fighter, they like all those things. So you can see where the real success lies. It's in the mental preparation. There are other factors that may come in later like genetic gifts, muscle twitch fibers, but that's 20%, and that's undeterminable. Their absorption of a hard shot, and their reaction to a hard shot, such as if a fighter's bell got rung and they went down, their reaction when that occurs, sometimes you can't fix that. Some things I can't change, but then there are other things that I can physically change. For example, with Jared (Mike's referring to his fighter Jared Gordon), with him if you look at the genetic makeup of his parents and brothers, he's really supposed to be a fat kid. What he's done is physically transform himself through hard work. With him I've tried to physically mold him to make up for his genetic deficiencies. Looking at this from the perspective of owning a business, there's no difference. I have big short-comings on a lot of different things. I don't have an attention span to stay too long on one task if it doesn't interest me, but I'm really good at creating ideas. So I look for people to compensate for my deficiencies and surround myself with these people. I understand what I'm good at and what I'm not good at and that requires me to be very honest with myself. Some things I can improve on by myself, some things I need to hire help for. That's how I've had success in business."

I agree with Mike on the importance of the mental aspect in fighting and in business, it is huge! This is something that can make or break you as a fighter or a business owner. Own the mental part of the game and constantly improve on it. Work on it like your profession depends on it, because in all reality it does!

My next question for Mike was a tough one: "If it came down to one characteristic that determines whether a fighter becomes a world champion, what is that characteristic?" Mike prefaced his answer by stating that we would have to assume that this fighter already has the physical characteristics of a championship fighter. Mike answered by stating the one characteristic he values the most, "The guy that'll separate themselves and establish themselves as champion is the man that can problem solve under incredible pressure at an extremely high rate." Mike went on to explain a situation where he simulated high pressure to get a fighter ready for a fight. "I have a fighter that has that problem of underperforming when there's high pressure. I realized the problem early on and decided we needed to fix it. So with him I tell him certain positions are just unacceptable. He got into a bad habit of letting people touch hands. I need to change him at a different level mentally to where he does not accept being touched. So if somebody even grazes him, he pulls back. In football, some coaches do this with their players that have 'fumbleitis' and fumble the ball a lot. The football coach will make the player walk with the ball all the time and random teammates will see the athlete and try to knock the ball out the player's hands. So the player that's carrying the ball, his muscles start twitching and reacting to hold on to that ball. Soon it becomes a new habit. It's the same principle I apply with my fighters when I need them to change. My fighter is really accepting of this tactic so in the past year we've had tremendous growth. The other thing I do is under time constraints I give him a task to complete. I might give him a really good brown belt and tell him 'You've got a minute to pass his guard.' He finally gets by, then we start shortening the clock, 45 seconds, then 30 seconds. Finally it's two guard passes in 20 seconds. He passes, then boom you've got another one, three guard passes in 20 seconds. I keep pushing the limits to where he can't fathom how he's going to get it done but I give him no alternative. The guy will be like '10 seconds? How am I going to pass?!' and I say 'So what, you're ready to give up? No? Show me!' He says, 'All right' and I count down, Nine! Eight! Seven! Six! Five! Four! So then I start seeing him go crazy like a hungry dog, and he'll get by, he'll pass the guard. And now it becomes habit. So now we go back to the principle of habits which also applies to business. Champions are created by the repetition of good habits."

Mike's belief of this principle of good habits is transferable when he explains it because it is understandable, and he describes it clearly with a lot of passion. He never once says it is easy but he makes it seem possible that anyone can replace bad habits with good habits through hard work and dedication. Mikes principle is simple. Success depends on the formation of good habits.

Mike then elaborated on some of the techniques he uses to get fighters to think differently. "With my pro fighters, the high level dudes, I tell them 'You were slow on the read.' What it means is the fighter missed an opportunity to advance their position against their opponent. It's often a small detail like hand positioning but in a high pressure situation against another elite fighter, that guy may have taken advantage and escaped. My fighters recognize this when I point it out, they understand when I tell them they were slow to make a positional transfer to stay in a dominant position. It's the little tiny details that matter the most at the highest level in the sport. "Things like placement of their posts, bodyweight distribution, and the details that were missed by the fighter. These are the things we'll discuss, and I continue to ask them to take detailed notes. The notes, the constant drilling and repetition, these are the things that form good habits. Once you start forming these habits at a subconscious level, the fighters no longer think about the actions needed to succeed against their opponents. Now the fighter no longer reads his opponents, he reacts before he reads. When I see my fighters reading their opponents, I tell them, using terminology that they understand, 'The mind is reading before the muscle,' then I say, 'I need the muscle to read before the mind.' In a high pressure situation where the movements are happening so fast, I need the muscle twitch fibers to react before the mind. If I visually have to see the movement, it's too late. I need the body to feel the twitch and react before the mind even has time to think. Then the mind will accommodate and let the body take over. It usually happens after years and years of repetition. Sometimes, depending on the fighters' age we may not have years and years. So that's where the note taking and attention to detail helps. We're trying to form deep grooves in the mind at a subconscious level."

I agree with Mike that notetaking can be a tremendous help, and to be competent the note taker must be engaged in wanting to learn and improve. The attention to detail using visual imagery can be an effective way to improve your skill in any arena. People who practice in their minds use the same circuitry as when they practice physically, the mind does not determine the difference. Therefore paying attention to detail and improving in your mind is just as important as practicing techniques using physical repetition.

Mike also explained the similarities between business and fighting. "Business and fighting are so similar. It's having those really good habits, writing things down and rereading your notes. I need to ask myself, 'Where did I fail and how do I improve?' If we're really breaking down the tiniest of details and a year goes by, there's no way I remember all those details, and I have to go back. I have to see if I fixed the errors. If I didn't fix it then there is no improvement. I have to work on my weakest areas. It's the same in fighting as in business. In business I know I need help with organization and scheduling. I have certain strengths. I'm great with customers, I'm great with selling, I'm great at creating ideas, and I know how to put a team together. I'm not great with creating a schedule or administration so I bring in people that are great in those areas and they help me. I know my strengths and weaknesses and I have to acknowledge them and look for where I can maximize my strengths and improve on my weaknesses."

Mike was great at connecting the similarities between fighting and business because he has proven to be very good at both pursuits. He has been a high level MMA trainer, Black Belt Brazilian Jiu-Jitsu practitioner and coach, and he has also been a very good businessman, having owned and operated several successful businesses. Mike utilized his philosophy of creating good habits in both fighting and in business. He has understood that the mental aspect is huge in each endeavor and he sought to instill replicable traits in himself and those that he coached.

Mike was also great at identifying his own strengths and weaknesses, and that is not easy to do. Being able to ask for help is also not easy, and I commend Mike for his ability to do so. Not everyone would be willing to admit, let alone seek assistance, for a perceived weakness. Mike's lack of ego allowed him to do what he did best and develop a team that provided him the support he needed to be successful. I would venture to guess that Mike's lack of ego is an attribute he developed as a Martial Artist, specifically a Brazilian Jiu-Jitsu practitioner. Getting as far as Mike has gotten as a BJJ competitor and coach requires no ego, just a love for the art and willingness to learn. This is a trait that I believe has helped Mike in his business endeavors.

I then asked Mike a question about motivation. I believed that a good leader not only motivates but also inspires people to take action. I knew that motivating someone after a tough loss, or while they're in the midst of adversity, is one of the hardest things to do as a coach. I wanted to understand how this high level coach motivated his fighters. So I asked Mike, "When the going gets rough in the ring, how do you motivate your fighters?" Mike thought about it for a few seconds and then answered, "I know guys will scream and yell 'You got to dig deep! You got to do this, you got to do that!' but that doesn't work, it just doesn't work. If the habits haven't been formed, then it's tough. There are certain things I look for to determine if my fighter is tired. Because as the saying goes 'Fatigue makes cowards of us all.' I don't like the term 'coward,' because a man is not a coward if he steps in that ring. I notice if a fighter is tired when I see them do the static hold. They'll get really tired and they get to a position that they feel safe in and they hold. That's when I tell them they need to practice good fundamentals and rely on their technique. I don't need safe I need them to win. When I start seeing that they're really tired I'm encouraging them so they're not simply holding, I need them to go fight even more, especially if they're in a bad position. I do that by changing their mindset, and that doesn't occur at fight time. The homework has to be done before fight time. You have to coach to the personality. Some guys have the trait where you can tell them what they need to do during fight time, and they go in and execute. Some guys have a trait where they train a certain way for a fight and then they go in and try to become a different fighter, something that they're not. So what I need from my fighters the most is fundamentals, technique, and attention to details. That comes from constantly working on it before the fight, molding these good habits. So in short, to answer the question, motivation does not happen in the ring, it's in training."

I thought about Mike's answer to my question about motivation. I noticed that as part of our culture we tend to romanticize motivation. We may look at a movie and see the coach yelling at his fighter between rounds, or giving a speech during half time, or the sales manager getting his team pumped up during a sales meeting. Whatever glorified Hollywood scene you may relate to (I too have these images in my head when I think of motivation), as a society we tend to look at motivation as something of a spark that can ignite us into action. In reality, hard work and training before the big event is what provides the best motivation. When we know we are prepared, ready, and willing to do our best, our success is much more attainable. We must not look to be motivated the day of the event. Motivation is something that is cultivated over time. This is what Mike believes in wholeheartedly and why he is so focused on creating good habits. All the motivation we need is within us if we are truly ready to do battle! Motivation is developed day in and day out by training the body and the mind to perform at the highest level. A good coach knows this and will help prepare his fighter so that the day of the event there is very little motivation needed, only direction, it is up to the fighter to take action. The work has been done and the fighter knows his potential, he must trust his training and focus his energy on the task, which is to win the fight.

My last question for Mike was one that I knew might be tough to answer, but I felt it needed to be answered for the purpose of knowing what was really important to Mike as a coach. I asked Mike "Who is the best fighter you ever coached, and why?" Mike answered, "The best fighter I ever coached was not my direct student, I was part of his fight teams and I did have input in helping him as a training partner and drilling partner as he was coming up. He was coached by my instructor, John Danaher. The fighter was George St. Pierre. Before he ever became UFC champion he was brought to Renzo Gracie's academy, and we would spend hours and hours together with John Danaher as John taught. That was part of my foundation and introduction to the sport of MMA. George and I spent a lot of time together, and he is the best fighter I ever saw for a couple of reasons. First and foremost, his work ethic is outrageous! He has what appears to be a photographic memory. Sometimes you think a person is so gifted because they remember everything, but that's bullshit! They're just so driven to succeed that they don't want to lose any information, they fight to remember everything. They write everything down. It's not just a photographic memory, they work at it. With George, he worked unbelievably hard, he wrote everything down, he was very detailed, and then when it came to fighting he had a game plan. He understood his strengths and weaknesses, he was incredibly honest with himself, even while in the ring under extreme pressure. He never deviated from his plan. I've seen UFC caliber fighters, where we've had great training camps, then during the fight, in the second or third round when a little fatigue comes in, they're doing moves that we've never done before, and I'm wondering what the hell they're doing! That never occurred with George. There was a system he understood and he practiced good habits on a daily basis. George is the best problem solver I've seen under extreme pressure where I've been personally involved. Another fighter that I admire is Khabib Nurmgomedov, he is the best one I've seen come along in a long time who is on that level."

I appreciated Mike's answer to my last question and even though Mike was not George St. Pierre's direct coach, his involvement was intensive and my intuition tells me that George benefited from training with Mike. The time that he and George spent training together had a lasting impression on Mike as a fighter and coach. Mike mentioned the attention to detail George had, and in his auto-biographical book, "The Way of the Fight," George describes how he would travel from Montreal Canada to the Renzo Gracie academy in New York City by bus every weekend to get his training in. He would take the 6-hour plus bus ride every weekend while he was working and training full-time to fulfill his dream of becoming a UFC champion. There is no doubt that he was dedicated to his craft and the way Mike explains how George had this incredible attention to detail, makes a lot of sense considering he was traveling 6 hours to train. George was most likely getting the most he could out of his training by taking explicitly detailed notes on every technique he was exposed to. The fact that most of us do not have to travel like George did to train in our craft, does not exclude us from the responsibility we have to make sure we are getting the most out of our training. If we implement the same sort of attention to detail, note taking, and dedication to anything we want to accomplish, our chances of success will dramatically improve.

Learn from your Experience – Key Points:

- The best education comes from the school of hard knocks. There is no substitute for real life experience. The sooner you start your real life education, the better.
- You are never "your own boss." In business you will always have a customer, and you work for that person. Service should be at your core.
- Be willing to change. Longevity in any field requires the ability to adapt and stay relevant.
- Don't settle for "safe" but reach for success. Success depends on you getting out your comfort zone.
- Dreams are just dreams unless you put in the work.
- Keep a journal and document your progress. You will determine what steps need to be taken on a subconscious level.
- Surround yourself with people that make up for your weaknesses. They will also complement your strengths.
- Champions are created by the intentional repetition of good habits.
- The details matter, and the higher you go, the more they matter.
- Motivation doesn't just happen on event day, it happens in training for the event. The more prepared you are, the more motivated you will be to perform.

Chapter 7: Capitalize on the Opportunity

Kipp Kollar is the owner of NAGA (North American Grappling Association), a submission grappling tournament organization, and Reality Fighting, a Mixed Martial Arts organization. As Matt Bessette and Jose Rivera explained in previous chapters, Kipp was their mentor when they first started their fight careers. Kipp has mentored and trained many fighters starting out in the MMA fight game, particularly those in the New England area. Kipp still trains with MMA fighters in what is officially known as Kipp's Basement, literally the basement of his house in Marlborough Connecticut. Most people who are involved in MMA in the New England area have witnessed or at least heard of Kipp's Basement.

I had the opportunity to speak with Kipp and his wife Mary to learn how Kipp started his company and what similarities he sees between the worlds of fighting and business, since Kipp has literally merged both these worlds. Kipp has a black belt in Tae Kwon Do, and a purple belt in Brazilian Jiu-Jitsu (although he has 20-plus years of grappling experience, he has not had any real affiliation to a BJJ school/coach in order to be given a higher ranking). Kipp also fought in 4 professional MMA fights and has a 4-0 record. Before and partly during starting NAGA, Kipp was a sales executive selling professional services in Manhattan, N.Y. Kipp taught Tae Kwon Do to executives at the insurance company he worked at, and that is how he started his entrepreneurial path. Kipp fought in point Karate tournaments all over New England and eventually started his own point Karate tournament as well as his own Tae Kwon Do school.

Kipp said that his interest in grappling started when he saw a poster on a wall at one of his friend's schools. It said, "'The Gracie $100,000 challenge.' Basically if you attended the seminar, fought the instructor, and beat him, he'll pay you $100,000." It was a Rickson Gracie seminar, Rickson was a Black Belt in Brazilian Jiu-Jitsu and undefeated in No-Holds-Barred fighting. Kipp and his friend who were both top Martial Arts competitors at the time decided to go to the seminar and take their shot against Rickson. The seminar was at a Jeet Kun Do school in Milford, CT. Kipp recalls "all of the grappling techniques I learned that day were new to me and I fumbled through each one while Rickson flowed like water from technique to technique." At the end of the technique portion of the seminar, Kipp remembers Rickson telling the attendees "If you really want to win the hundred grand I want to go with you first, raise your hand," and Kipp admits with a smile that he did not raise his hand. Kipp remembers "The first three guys were just there for the money, and he (Rickson) basically murdered them! He (Rickson) said 'You ready? Ok let's go!' The first guy was a 240-pound wrestler, he shot in and Rickson flipped him over catching him in a foot lock, making him tap from pain in a matter of seconds. It didn't matter what these guys threw at Rickson, he ended each match effortlessly with some type of submission hold. The instructor who ran the seminar was Rick Manatee, who was a good grappler, so he lasted the longest of anybody in attendance. Rickson didn't try to submit him right away, he kind of had fun with him. So I was like, 'Ok I get this, don't try to punch him in the face, and he won't rip your head off (laughs).' So we grappled for a bit, I didn't try to punch him because I knew I wasn't going to win. But after that seminar I thought, 'That was awesome; we've got to learn more about jiu-jitsu and grappling.' It had to be like 1992, so this was my first introduction to grappling."

As Kipp explained his initial interest in grappling I felt like I was there with him because the story was so vivid. "Over time, I became friends with him (Rickson). We spoke on the phone, and I'd ask him 'where can I get videos?' but the reality was that Rickson lived in California and I lived in Connecticut, and the distance was far too great for me to master his art. Then I met Joe Cuff at a Renzo Gracie seminar in New York City. Joe had tons of videos. One of them was made by Kazeka Muniz, he was a blue belt from Brazil. I watched his tape probably 100 times practicing the moves and becoming proficient at them. It's kind of funny he fought a NAGA like 20 years later, I saw his name listed as a competitor at our Las Vegas competition. By then he was a black belt so I asked him, 'Did you make a video when you were a blue belt? He said yes, and I said, 'I owe you because I learned everything I know about jiu-jitsu from that video (laughs).' Realistically, I knew it would take years and years to acquire the level of skill that Rickson, Renzo, and Kazeka possessed."

Kipp went on, "While seminars and videos existed for grappling, one thing I noticed was that there were no grappling competitions. So I added a single grappling division to my annual point karate tournament. We had one weight class, one skill level and one mat. Our only advertisement was word of mouth and we had 40 grapplers sign up and compete that day. The wrestlers won the first one. They were just good at taking people down and holding them there. They (wrestlers) didn't know what it was, we just explained the rules and they did their best to comply by the rules we created. At the conclusion of the event competitors were chomping at the bit asking, 'When's the next tournament?' When you run a karate tournament, you do it once a year. Basically instructors run these events to raise money for their academies. It's customary for instructors to support each other's annual events. We had a network of instructors that did this. These events were run primarily by volunteers – i.e. our friends – and to be quite honest most events were extremely unprofessional. Adding the grappling division just added to the chaos. We were making things up as we went along – if you get a takedown it's a point, if you go for a submission attempt it's a point. We created points that could be earned during the match so a winner could be determined if no submissions were achieved. And back then we didn't do any Gi; it was just NoGi. Eventually we added Gi because a lot of people wanted to do Gi, and initially we used the same rules. We learned over time that people don't want our rules for Gi, they want the IBJJF rules (the IBJJF is the International Brazilian Jiu-Jitsu Federation). So over time, we added Gi divisions and changed it to the IBJJF rules vs NAGA rules for Gi because it increased the overall number of competitors. That's how it all started."

I asked Kipp if he was making a profit from his Point Karate tournaments before he incorporated grappling. He explained, "Yes, the Point Karate tournament was a great moneymaker for our program. I got the idea from a family friend named Liz Frillici, a dance instructor. Liz told me that she made more money at her one annual recital, than she made all year from tuition, because of all the spectators and food and parking etc. All of your training and practice leads up to that one event and it is very important to all those involved so that once a year when you run a tournament you have all these other schools and spectators that come that pay, and they buy outfits, entrance fees, concessions etc. Students and families are willing to pay significant sums of money on an event like this. The only problem with Liz's formula is that the payday came only once a year. It was very similar to the Point Karate tournaments. In Point Karate, you can only do them once a year because if you went more than once a year people didn't come because they considered you greedy. But grappling was new, there were no other tournaments anywhere so people were like 'When's the next tournament?' and I'd be like 'A year from now,' and people said 'You got to have more than one tournament a year, because no one else does this.' So when in six months I did another tournament, the Point Karate dropped dramatically, but the grappling went up. In six months, it went up again, it doubled every time. And then we stopped doing the Point Karate tournaments completely, because first of all it wasn't real, second of all the grappling was so much more popular. It was getting bigger and bigger and bigger. Think about any new sport that came along during your lifetime – snowboarding, windsurfing – they don't come along that often, but if you're at the entry level of a new sport and you're the one running a tournament around it, then there's a huge potential for success. So that's how we started NAGA. In the meantime, I had a sales job like you currently have (referring to me), working as many hours as you do. Our first child was born the month I moved away from my full-time job and started NAGA, and it was rough, very rough at first."

I admire Kipp for doing what he did because as I start my own business and write this book I am experiencing the juggling act that Kipp was referring to when he stated

"It was rough." I know the dedication and time it takes to undertake any project of significance. For Kipp, it was starting NAGA, which has grown to be one of the most recognized grappling tournaments in the United States and is continuing to grow worldwide. Kipp applied the concepts he learned from Martial Arts to business and *made* Martial Arts his business. His dedication and persistence enabled him to be as successful as he is today in business.

I asked Kipp what similarities he saw between martial arts/fighting and business and how his martial arts training may have helped him in business. He explained, "When I started Tae Kwon Do, I was a college freshman. I always wanted to do it, I was a swimmer before that, but I always wanted to do some kind of fighting. You know everybody gets bullied, so like most people I wanted to put an end to it. Tae Kwon Do classes were held every Monday through Friday 90 minutes a day. I had 122 people start as white belts in my Tae Kwon Do class; when I graduated college I was the only one in that initial group who got a black belt. To me, it's the same in Martial Arts training as in business. Everybody wants to make a lot of money, everybody wants their black belt, everybody wants to be successful, but it's the few that put in the hard work that persevere. When you're trying to get a college education and you do the Tae Kwon Do on the side, when you have a full time job and a wife and kids, and you're trying to support your family with your full time job and you want to do the sport on the side...how hard is that to get your black belt? You have to do the work and many times go above and beyond what is expected of you." I dug a little deeper by asking for specific characteristics Kipp could share with us. Things that he himself received from training Tae Kwon Do and have helped him in business. He answered with "Self-initiative and common sense. All the things that you learn in college, I have to do well in college, I'm by myself, I'm a young kid, there's all these other things that can pull me away from studying. There's drinking, there's smoking, there's partying. All these things pull you from your main objective which is to study and do well in school. In the professional world, life has its distractions as well. Being able to juggle family, career and then taking on a second career is a tremendous feat. Learning from your mistakes, taking risks, and following through aren't just words. They are a lifestyle that most people who lack discipline cannot adhere to."

I switched the topic a bit with my next question and focused more on fighting and the fighting mindset. I asked Kipp "Which fighters do you admire most and why?" Kipp answered, "I'm not going to give you names, I'm going to give you the type of fighter that I admire because I have many friends that fight that are personal friends so if I talk about them I'd be biased. I like fighters that when they lose, they don't make excuses." Kipp went on to speak with me about a fighter we both know that recently lost his pro fight in the UFC, and a conversation he had with that particular fighter. "He told me before his fight that he had a torn meniscus. He didn't bring that up in his post-fight interview. Most fighters have injuries just from training, so they're all in that same boat. But I don't like when fighters make excuses when they lose. I don't like when the fighters blame the judges when it's a close fight, because his (Kipp's friend) fight was close. I like what he (Kipp's friend) said: 'I didn't submit him, I didn't knock him out, I can give you my opinion of the fight, I thought I threw more punches and kicks that landed, but he controlled me more on the ground. Some judges think ground control is more important, some judges think that stand up is more important.' At the end of the day, I like fighters that are honest and genuine and come back from losses. A lot of fighters will come back from a loss and do the exact same thing. Other fighters will come back from a loss and say 'That guy took me down five times in one round' and they learn more wrestling. They may have been the better striker, but instead of just working on their striking they went back and learned more wrestling. I admire the fighters that acknowledge their weaknesses and then improve upon them. In the fight world that's really hard to do. For example, when you're a college Division 1 wrestler and you're in an MMA match, it's really hard not to go back to your core strength. This is what your opponent expects. Intelligent, successful fighters, like Frankie Edgar who was a very good college wrestler from New Jersey, he'll go through five championship rounds and never take the other guy down, at all. He wins the fight from striking. These are the kinds of fighters that I admire."

I took this to mean that Kipp admires fighters that can overcome a loss or adversity, with no excuses. He likes fighters that can change strategies and adapt their styles to be different from what an opponent might expect. In business, it's the same – no excuses, overcome adversity, adapt and excel. These characteristics can be the difference makers for a successful business and a successful business person. Kipp himself was able to apply these principles to making NAGA a business success.

I went back to speaking with Kipp about his business dealings and how he has been able to flourish and thrive in the business of Martial Arts. To me, time management is essential to business success, so I asked him, "How do you prioritize your time to maximize results?" Kipp answered, "A long, long time ago when I was the only employee of NAGA, it was extremely difficult. I had a high pressure sales job, a wife who had just had our first child and was on maternity leave. Then I had this hobby that I wanted to turn into my primary source of income. You have your family that should be your number one priority. Having a hard-working, supportive spouse makes all the difference in the world. I had quarterly sales quotas from my sales job that had to be met or they would get rid of me. So ultimately in the beginning your hobby or passion that you want to turn into a business becomes last, and that is what makes it so difficult to succeed. I remember nights working on sales presentations until 7 p.m., then starting in on NAGA work, staying up until 1 or 2 a.m. Then leaving for the office again at 7 a.m. to start the cycle all over again."

Kipp continued, "Once I left my sales job, I was able to focus in on my new career. Over time, what I've learned is that if you hire good people and you take care of good people they will take care of you, and then you don't have to do everything yourself. And it's the hardest thing when you hire somebody and they're not good to get rid of them, and when you hire somebody who's really good to reward them, because if you're greedy you just want to keep them at a minimum rate. A good company owner will always reward those people that are exceptional, they'll get rid of the ones that are below average, and they'll coach the ones that are average, hopefully to be better."

I then asked Kipp about goal setting, specifically probing for how he sets his goals and measures them. Kipp said, "It's funny because initially NAGA and the IBJJF were the only two players in town, and over time we kept continuing to grow. My wife works for United Healthcare, she has to deal with companies like Aetna, The Hartford, all these others professional companies, where NAGA initially didn't have to deal with any other professional companies. There were other instructors that were black belts trying to run Jiu-Jitsu tournaments or grappling tournaments that would have their friends and family work for free, but we were paying people, and we were doing it every weekend. We had training; if they weren't good we got rid of them, if they were good we promoted them, so it was a real company. My goal for NAGA was to provide a professional tournament with professional referees and a management team for each event that would ensure a fair unbiased platform to compete. Now people have caught on 25 years later. It's easy to copy what someone else does. After a while people started copying our blueprint. The guy who started Grapplers Quest (Grapplers Quest is a grappling tournament organization), worked for us not because he wanted to expand NAGA, he did it because he was copying what we did, he did it for like three years, then he started Grapplers Quest, and it was an exact duplicate of NAGA. Fortunately, he went out of business, bankruptcy, IRS problems...Karma's a bitch! Today there are more intelligent people that are my competitors now, doing what we do, offering lower prices, so we competitively have to think of new things to be better than them. Ultimately it comes down to customer service, in any business, doesn't matter where you are, a restaurant, a gas station, a Jiu-Jitsu tournament, it's all about customer service. For what people are paying, as long as you treat them well, especially if they have problems, they'll come back."

I asked where Kipp sees NAGA going five years from now. I really wanted to get a glimpse of how he thinks and how his business mind works. He answered, "Our goal is to grow every year, have more competitors, have more tournaments, and obviously make more money. Originally, we were just in New England then we expanded across the country, we added Hawaii, we added Canada.

Then we bought a set of mats and we sent them out to Europe, and we have a company that ships throughout Europe, so now we do all of Europe. We're constantly expanding, most recently into South America. There are other countries like China, Australia that are on our road map. But expanding more doesn't always mean making more money. We can do a show in Italy and only have 200 competitors and lose ten grand. So you have to do your research and marketing and figure out if it's worthwhile. There are many reasons why an event is not successful in a foreign country. It is much more expensive to do a show in Europe than here. You have to do your research and predetermine if a foreign location will be worthwhile. In short, five years from now we want to continue to expand NAGA worldwide in those countries where it makes sense."

Kipp added what core beliefs direct his business now and in the future. "Right now we are really focusing more on 'Why would someone go to another tournament instead of ours? Or why do we mail, like flyers or posters, to a school and then they reject it and send it back to us?' There's all sorts of schemes like 'If you bring 25 students, we'll give you some money. If your school comes in first place, we'll give you some money. If we do a super fight, we'll pay your main instructor some money.' But they're all schemes. At the end of the day, people want to have good referees, they don't want to be cheated. From twenty four years of experience, we learned that all these little shortcuts don't work. At the end of the day, really good customer service is what, in any company, makes you profitable. Period."

My last intended question for Kipp was "What drives you?" I explained the response I was looking for by clarifying that I wasn't looking for motivation, or motivational quotes or anything like that, I was looking for a driving factor. I feel that drive and motivation are different, where motivation comes and goes, drive is more personal and stays with you. Kipp answered my question by explaining his driving force(s) "I think it's pretty simple, hard work pays off. If you want to become a black belt in a martial art, if you want to become really good at a sport, if you want to be senior vice president at an insurance company, if you want to run your own business, it always comes down to common sense, hard work, and self-motivation. And if you utilize those three things and you're successful, then financially you're rewarded, you reward your family from those benefits, and hopefully you pass that on to your family...so ultimately it just feels good. You work out, it's tough, and afterwards when you're healthy...it makes you feel good. When I stayed up until 2 a.m. working on a NAGA event and the turnout was double the prior event, it felt great." I then added, "Doing things that are hard make you feel good?" Kipp replied, "Right. Watching TV every night, drinking a beer, and sleeping 'til eleven..." I joked, "It's nice for one day, ha-ha." Kipp's wife, Mary, who was also there with us during the interview, added, "We don't sleep 'til eleven." Kipp noted, "Even on weekends we don't sleep 'til eleven, ever." Mary finished with, "We're up at least by eight." Although I was joking and being facetious when I said, 'It's nice for one day' referring to sleeping late, the Kollars did not agree with me, and I could see that getting up early was something they valued, as most successful people do. I appreciated the correction and took what was intended from the question. What drives Kipp is doing things that are difficult, like running an international grappling tournament organization, because ultimately, it feels good.

I asked Kipp for a recap on his history leading up to

where he is today. He recapped, "I graduated from Bryant University in 1987. I started working for Travelers' Insurance as a computer programmer, eventually became a project manager. I then left that company and went into sales, selling enterprise imaging systems to insurance companies as a district sales manager, and that's when I started NAGA. The entire time I was training and competing. I had my daughter, quit my job, and started NAGA (full time) when I was about thirty." Kipp's Tae Kwon Do tournaments that first incorporated grappling were called "Winter Whirlwind." Kipp recalls the first tournaments that incorporated grappling. "Renzo Gracie came, Ricardo Almeida and Matt Serra all attended, they won the team title. These are big names in the MMA and Grappling worlds. I was a UFC referee and judge, they paid me 250 bucks (laughs) to fly out to Vegas for a weekend, which just didn't cut it. The first NAGA without Tae Kwon Do was held at Wesleyan University; we had sixty competitors, two weight classes, and two skill levels." Reality fighting (Kipp's MMA fight company) was called "MASS Destruction" at first. "A boxing instructor from Pawtucket Rhode Island approached me at one of my grappling tournament, and he goes 'Kipp I hold boxing events in my gym. Would you like to do some grappling and Vale Tudo matches to add to my card?' Back then we didn't call it MMA, we called it Vale Tudo, which means "anything goes" in Portuguese. There were no government restrictions or regulations, so we just made up the rules and ran our first event. Fighters could use open hand strikes, because there were no MMA gloves back then, and you could knee, elbow and submit each other. Our first event attracted fighters like Tim Sylvia and Jorge Rivera. Tim Sylvia later became the UFC Heavyweight Champion, and Jorge Rivera also made a successful run in the UFC. There were no weight classes, so Jorge was 185 pounds, Tim Sylvia was like 260 pounds, and Jorge arm barred him

"That was the second show, first show they fought in separate fights and beat their own opponents, then they fought each other. When Tim and Jorge fought, the crowd went crazy, it was standing room only. Other big names that fought in those shows included Mike Brown, who was a UFC vet from ATT (American Top Team). The list goes on, Joe Lauzon, Kenny Florian, Frankie Edgar, the list goes on and on. These Vale Tudo fights were a separate business; it gave grapplers the opportunity to take it a step up and compete in what is today known as mixed martial arts. We created Mass Destruction to fill that void. To date, we have run over 200 of these events."

I asked which of the two, grappling or MMA, did he see his business heading toward. Kipp said "Reality Fighting and MASS Destruction, all the MMA shows, there's so much competition, it's very expensive, fighters drop out, and it's not a lucrative business unless you're the UFC. Really. That's why there is only the UFC. Grappling, on the other hand, consists of primarily amateurs; everyone pays to compete, and spectators pay. MMA requires additional expenses such as you have to pay the fighter purses, expensive advertising and venues. Many fighters don't have insurance, so you have to pay for their medicals (medical clearance). Currently we do two shows a year at Mohegan (Mohegan Sun Casino), and that's it. We used to do about twenty shows a year, and it's really dropped down because it's not a moneymaker, and it's a lot of work."

I understood what Kipp was saying. In business, if it's not a moneymaker, and it's a lot of work, plus you have another revenue stream that is making money, you naturally gravitate towards where the money is.

I really appreciated the time I had with Kipp. His ability to see the market opportunity in creating NAGA was extraordinary, but what I found even more impressive was how he capitalized on it. He did not think about it, he did it, he kept moving toward his goal. He simply started something that brought value to people and found better and better ways to do it as he went along. This is what separates Kipp from people who have good ideas, but just keep them as ideas. Kipp turned his idea into action, which is now a Reality (pun intended). With regards to fighting and business, Kipp took his persistence and dedication, which he learned from Tae Kwon Do and Grappling, and applied it to business by sticking with it. He had some rough times, as he admits, but he did not stop doing what he felt was necessary to keep his company going. Kipp is determined to stay ahead of the competition and find new ways to attract more competitors and keep NAGA growing worldwide. His training in Martial Arts will undoubtedly be helpful in beating the competition. There is no doubt in my mind, or Kipp's, that he will capitalize on the opportunity!

Capitalize on the Opportunity – Key Points:

- Find a Niche and Capitalize. If something is not being done that people want, start doing it, you will figure it out as you go along.
- Being at the beginning of something new increases your chances of success.
- Stick with it. Success comes from being able to persevere and grind it out when others won't.
- "Learning from mistakes, taking risks, and following through aren't just words. They are a lifestyle..."
- "Take care of good people and they will take care of you."
- "Really good customer service is what, in any com-

pany, makes you profitable. Period."

- Hard work pays off. And it makes you feel good.

Chapter 8: Create your Legacy

Rafael "Formiga" Barbosa is a Brazilian Jiu-Jitsu high level black belt competitor and is quickly becoming a living legend in the sport. He was given the nickname "Formiga" by his coach Andre "Dedeco" Almeida. Formiga means ant in Portuguese (Portuguese is the national language of Brazil, Rafael's native land). Rafael earned the nickname as a kid when he started training Brazilian Jiu-Jitsu because he was the smallest and youngest in his class at 11 years old. The nickname actually started as "Formiguinha" or little ant, then developed into "Formiga" as Rafael got older. Formiga went through the belt ranks of Brazilian Jiu-Jitsu with his coach Andre Almeida in Rio de Janeiro Brazil, eventually receiving his black belt from Almeida in 2002.

Formiga as of this writing was a five-time IBJJF world champion in the Master's division (the Master's division starts at 30 years of age), five-time IBJJF Pan Am champion in the Master's division, two-time Brazilian Champion in the Adult division (the Adult division is 18-29 years of age), three-time IBJJF world championship bronze medalist in the Adult division, and dozens upon dozens of wins in the IBJJF open championships. Formiga, along with some of his former teammates, went on to form a formidable Brazilian Jiu-Jitsu team known as Soul Fighters.[2] He continues to build on his accomplishments as an active competitor, coach, and lifetime student of Brazilian Jiu-Jitsu.

Formiga's nickname, which means "ant," is often thought to be given to him because of his unusually strong legs, which he uses to sweep his opponents from bottom position to get on top and control them. Ants have incredible strength for their size so people often think that's how he got his nickname. But in actuality, it was just what his coach called him when he was the smallest guy in the training room, "little ant." The name stuck, and it suits him well. He uses his power very effectively and efficiently, just like an ant. You won't see Formiga wasting energy or trying to use too much strength during his fights. He is all about leverage and timing. What looks like power is actually years of refined technique.

I wanted to know how Formiga handled transitioning from Brazil to the United States to become a professional athlete, coach and co-founder of the Soul Fighters team. Formiga explained the transition by stating "When I started Jiu-Jitsu it was all about just having fun. It was not my goal to become a Jiu-Jitsu pro and make money. When I started to realize that I'm already a pro, I was a teenager training four times a day, lifting weights and conditioning myself, all because I just wanted to get better at Jiu-Jitsu. Then the doors started to open for me because I started to get good, I put a lot of time on the mats. Nothing was given to me, I trained hard and I made it happen, not because I wanted to be a pro, just because I wanted to get better. I just fell in love with Jiu-Jitsu from day one. My first five years of Jiu-Jitsu I never missed one class, it's crazy, not one class. Everything I could do to be on the mats I would do it because I loved it so much. And it's still my love. Every time I go on vacation I take my Gi (the Gi also known as the kimono is the traditional Jiu-Jitsu uniform) and wherever I'm going I train because I love Jiu-Jitsu. My wife says, 'That's your job, why do you want to train on vacation?' and I say no, my job is teaching Jiu-Jitsu, training Jiu-Jitsu is my passion! One day I came here to Connecticut to teach a seminar after the IBJJF Pan Am tournament, and Matt (Matthew Bryers, owner of Jiu-Jitsu Strength Academy or JSA in Cromwell CT) came up to me and offered me an opportunity to teach at his academy and I accepted. I didn't even know how to speak any English at that point, but I decided to try it anyway. In my first year in Connecticut, I didn't know anything, not even how to say, 'Hi how are you?' but I just tried and slowly learned by talking with people as best I could. It was really hard at first, but with time I started to learn and get better and better. I started to understand and people started helping me more. Little by little I learned English and now I understand it and people can understand me, especially when I'm talking Jiu-Jitsu, I can explain everything really well. Now this is my life, I don't want to go back to Brazil, I love it here in the U.S., and this is where I want my kids to grow up. Because of my success as a competitor, my student base has grown and I have people coming to train with me from all over. The competitions have been a free form of advertising myself. Before I left to Texas (a recent move) to teach, we grew to seven affiliates between Connecticut and New York with almost a thousand students between the seven academies! It's incredible because when I first got here I didn't have anything and I didn't know anybody, just Matt. My first class we had fifteen guys on the mat, and we grew slowly; now eight years later we have a thousand students under the Soul Fighters name in Connecticut and New York."

I noticed a few lessons in Formiga's explanation of the

transition from Brazil to the United States and from student to professional athlete/teacher. The main thing I recognized was that Formiga followed his passion. He simply loves Jiu-Jitsu and wanted to get better. The pursuit of his passion to get better at Jiu-Jitsu opened all the doors he needed to build a successful following as a world class athlete and coach. Although he self admittedly did not plan his success, his commitment to the art he loves and his dedication to his craft eventually provided the success he needed to continue following his passion and make a living doing so. It's an amazing example of what following your heart, hard work, and commitment can do for us.

My next question for Formiga was with regards to his competition success. Although his professional success was not necessarily planned, I wanted to know what he envisioned for the competitions he entered. So I asked him if he had specific goals for the competitions. He answered, "Yes, I had two goals when I first started Jiu-Jitsu. I wanted to become a Black Belt, and I accomplished that, I got my Black Belt in 2002, I was 19 years old. And then I wanted to become a world champion as a Black Belt in the Adult division, that goal I never achieved, and it's probably not going to happen because I'm not competing in that division anymore. I'm not frustrated with not achieving that goal even though for so long it was my goal. I was right there all along, three times I got third place at worlds, and I lost to the champion by 1 advantage (an advantage is part of the IBJJF scoring system, and although it's not considered a point, if a match is tied on points the competitor with more advantages wins). All three times I was really close, but it never happened. Still I am happy. I have made a name for myself in Jiu-Jitsu and I'm considered one of the best butterfly guard players in all of Jiu-Jitsu."

In Formiga's case of not achieving his goal of becoming

a world champion in the Adult division, I believe it actually made him more competitive and hungry to keep competing. Although he did not become a world champion in the Adult division, he became a world champion in the Masters Division several times over, and he shows no signs of slowing down! He has effectively cemented his name as one of the best Brazilian Jiu-Jitsu competitors of all time. Formiga explained, "I'm 36, and I see a lot of people my age that just don't want to compete anymore; it's crazy because I want to compete more and more and more! My wife asked me why I keep competing, and being honest I answered because if I don't keep competing I don't think I want to be on the mats anymore. Competing keeps me training; it keeps me hungry to learn more and teach more and make others better as well." So you can see that the fire still burns in Formiga's belly, and for him competition is what keeps that fire burning. Ask yourself this question, "What keeps me hungry?" Answering that question to will keep your fire burning as well.

Formiga being a top level competitor and coach, it seemed to me that finding mentors and coaches might be somewhat difficult for Formiga. I asked him who he goes to for advice and coaching. He answered, "That's a good question. At some point you start to know more than your coach. My coach 'Dedeco' taught me everything that I know to help me build my foundation. As my game evolved, I noticed his game is different than mine. I started to develop my own game, and then he can't give me as much advice because that's not his game. The same thing happens with me and my students. So we started to have clinics. We sit down with like 10 black belts on the mats, and problem solve together, we each may have trouble with certain positions, so we discuss them. Each one has a different view on a technique, and each one has different application of a technique. So we get different views, and we can decide which approach works best for us. In that way, we learn together. The clinics with other black belts and maybe some high level brown belts will help you more than having one coach tell you what you need to do. After you get your black belt, you need to open up your mind, pay attention, and figure out what works best for you." I equate Formiga's black belt clinics to a "mastermind group." The "mastermind group" is one of the 13 principles described in the timeless classic book by Napoleon Hill titled "Think and Grow Rich." The principle of the "mastermind group" is that collectively a group of high performers is stronger than any one individual. By creating a collective conscious each member is able to benefit from the group's experience, expertise, and energy. The "mastermind group" is used to expand one's views, knowledge, and resources, and achieve goals faster and more efficiently. This is exactly what Formiga is describing when he talks about the black belt clinics. He is using the clinics as a learning tool and a resource to achieve his goal of getting better at Jiu-Jitsu. Although Napoleon Hill described the "mastermind group" in reference to business, this is a concept that Formiga has applied to Jiu-Jitsu. And it is a concept that has served many people well, whether they be fighters or business people, the "mastermind group" is a phenomenal tool for progress and self-development.

As he spoke more about the concept of the black belt clinics, Formiga became more excited and explained this concept in further detail "Once you get your black belt, you're able to say 'Ok that position is great, but it's not for me. Or that position is good and it's going to fit in my game, I just need to practice it over and over and over and it will become part of my game too.' After I got my black belt, I learned this strategy (the black belt clinics). I got my black belt in 2002, and in 2006 my coach came to the U.S. After only four years of being a black belt, I had nobody to coach me, and I freaked out, but that's how I learned to get better, through trial and error, and I feel that I started to learn way more! I think about it like this, when you're in school you learn a little bit about everything. That's when you're a blue belt, purple belt, and brown belt. Then when you get your black belt you just got into college. In college you decide on what path you will take, such as becoming an engineer. Now you study mostly engineering. That's exactly what happens when you get your black belt, now you want to know more about your game. Of course, you still need to know a little bit of everything, because you need to escape positions etc. but you will specialize in your game. At that point, you need different views of your game. For example, a lot of people say my game is really close to Marcelo Garcia (Marcelo Garcia is one of the best grapplers of all time and another Brazilian Jiu-Jitsu legend). Marcelo and I are friends, but we never had the chance to get on the mat together where we could exchange ideas. I wish we would because I know I would learn a lot and he would learn from me. I would get a look at how he understands certain positions and he would see how I understand certain techniques. We could play the same game, but we will see it through different eyes."

With that last statement Formiga explained a beautiful concept: "Playing the same game but seeing it through different eyes" is not only empowering but mind expanding. Whatever your profession or craft, taking the time to learn from and exchange ideas with other high performers in your area of expertise is a game changer. Formiga describes it as a necessity and the only way he was able to take his game to the next level. Take this concept and make it your own to elevate your game as well.

Challenges and obstacles are something we all face and can grow from, so I asked Formiga which challenges he has had that he learned from the most? Formiga answered, "I learned from my first competition that when you lose you actually *win* more than when you win. What that means is that when you lose a competition, the day after the match you're going to realize all the mistakes you made from the first step on. Maybe it was a certain grip, and my opponent was able to break that grip, pass my leg, etc. You're going to be able to notice the details when you lose a match, but when you win you don't remember anything because you just did your job. In my opinion when you win you don't learn anything new. When you lose, you're learning new ways to deal with the mistakes you made. You may take a week, a month, or a year to work on fixing those mistakes so they don't happen again. What I learned from competing I apply to my whole life, every time I fail I need to learn from it so it doesn't happen again. I was 11 years old when I did my first competition and I still use that idea of learning from my mistakes my whole life. When I mess up with my wife, I can't let it happen again. When I mess up with my job, I can't let it happen again. The same thing goes for my family and so on. I'm always learning. Every time I fail, I need to learn from my mistakes, and fix my mistakes."

I was surprised by how Formiga, being such a high-level competitor and multiple time world champion, was so comfortable with using the word "fail." He obviously viewed failure as part of the process. He had become a world champion many times over, despite the fact that he has failed along the way. He actually valued failure in that it seemed to be his greatest teacher. This was the mindset of a champion. Sure, we want to win and winning feels good. Losing sucks, but we must be okay with that from time to time because we must accept the risk. Getting comfortable with the idea that you might fail is the only way to succeed.

I asked Formiga what his next big goal was. He answered, "I have two goals. I just moved to Dallas, Texas, and I want to become the biggest academy in Dallas. There's one academy with 700 students; I want 750 students. I want to pass them. It's not for the money – of course, I want to make money – but I want to be the biggest like I am in Connecticut. I know by far that I'm the biggest BJJ association in Connecticut, and I want to do the same in Dallas. I want to keep growing the Soul Fighters association and spreading the Jiu-Jitsu life. In my opinion, Jiu-Jitsu is not just a martial art, it's a lifestyle, because from the time you start wanting to get better at Jiu-Jitsu you need to change your life a little bit. Diet will change, you're going to sleep earlier to wake up feeling better, and you're going to exercise more to train better. Something in your life will change, and when this happens that becomes the Jiu-Jitsu lifestyle. That's my goal, to bring more people into my lifestyle."

Whether or not this chapter inspires you to join the Jiu-Jitsu lifestyle – and I am a big advocate of this lifestyle – my hope is that you take the concepts described by Formiga and apply them to your life. We can all learn from the mindset of this champion. He is comfortable with failure because he realizes that occasional failure is the only way to be successful. He is training, competing, and growing his academies, fulfilling his passion for Jiu-Jitsu. He is loving what he does, all the ups and downs, the success, the failure, and the hard work. There is no complaining when things get rough because he knows setbacks are temporary. He stays his course. He puts everything he has into what he does and he is leaving his legacy. He succeeds because he gives himself the permission to fail, and the chance to win. You can do the same. Fulfill your passion and create your own legacy.

Create your Legacy – Key Points:

- Start by having fun. Do what you really enjoy doing. If you really enjoy it, the hard work required to be good at it won't seem so hard.
- When you're passionate about what you do, and you put in the hard work to become good at it, people will take notice. Opportunities will come because others in your field will gravitate towards you.
- Sometimes not reaching a goal will drive you to achieve more than you originally set out to do. When a goal is not achieved, there are other goals, sometimes bigger goals, still waiting for you.
- Find your fire. Whether it be competition, innovation, creation, or taking your business/career to the next level, find what drives you to get better. This will keep you in the game as long as that fire stays lit.
- Mastermind your way to success. Find other successful people and learn from them. In your field there are other people like you who want to improve. Seek them out, meet with them, exchange ideas, learn and grow together.
- Get comfortable with the idea that you might fail. Failure allows you to find out what needs to be improved so you can become the best at what you do.
- If it helps you, it can help others. What has helped you the most so far? Is it a lifestyle, a set of ideas, a set of values? Spread the knowledge because if you benefit from something, most likely others will too.

Chapter 9: Enjoy the Journey

My personal experience with fighting and business is that both require extreme focus and commitment in order to get the outcome you desire, which generally speaking is a WIN. Winning a fight is, in my opinion, very similar to winning a sale, a promotion, a new job, or a closing a deal. Let's face it, fighting is not meant to be easy, and if it's easy, it's because the preparation made it easy. If the preparation for a fight is way harder than the fight itself, you've put yourself in a great position to win. I've had the privilege of training Brazilian Jiu-Jitsu for over a decade, and I have also had the opportunity to compete along this journey. I've been fortunate to win several BJJ competitions by putting the concepts described in this book to practice. I've also felt the pain and disappointment from losses in competition, and I like the feeling of winning way better. That being said, win or lose, every competition is a learning experience like no other. I will continue to compete in Brazilian Jiu-Jitsu, focusing on the process and a good performance. In every competition, the more dedicated, focused, and physically fit I am, the better the outcome. Looking back on my successes as well as setbacks in BJJ competition, I can say that the mental aspect plays the biggest part. Commitment is usually the deciding factor for me achieving my successes. This is because commitment clears the mind of other possibilities. Early on in my sales career, I had a sales manager who once told me "*The absence of alternatives clears the mind absolutely.*" That statement has stuck with me ever since. So commitment leads to preparation, which leads to expectation. This is a powerful sequence that if applied with a plan and a purpose, will lead to success.

Success is the result of several actions executed properly. However, setbacks are a valuable tool as well. Setbacks are the best teachers because they allow us to realize the holes in our physical and mental preparation. Without setbacks, there can be no progress and growth. Therefore, I am learning to embrace setbacks as my teachers. Of course I want to win and I go in to competition with a winning mindset, however there is more to competing than winning, as cliché as that may sound. There are many reasons to compete but the most logical reason to me is to get better. Because intensity and focus increases with the anticipation of competition, I believe learning is heightened and this allows me to adapt more readily to the competitive mindset. As I train for and compete in BJJ tournaments, I feel that I push myself physically and mentally. The process of getting ready for competition, in and of itself, sharpens my skills. I put trust into my training, my coaches, my team, and my fighting spirit. This process applies to business as well. When getting ready for a big meeting or presentation, the preparation should involve diligent practice of the possible scenarios, either in your mind or played out with others. Play out as many good and bad scenarios as you can imagine and rehearse your response to each scenario so that the result is favorable to you. The more attention to detail and the more you practice your presentation, the more confidence you will build. The process should feel like progress but don't get discouraged if you often have to reassess and take a step back to then move two steps forward. That is part of the process. Progress does not always come as fast as we want it but it will eventually come when we put in the work. Practice with intent and purpose to get the most out of your training sessions. This applies to every situation where we have a defined goal. Most of all embrace the process, because in doing so you are growing as a person, and your consistent, purposeful training is making you a master at your craft.

Brazilian Jiu-Jitsu (BJJ) requires refined technique that only comes from a lot of repetition. A typical BJJ training session involves a warmup, drills, and then live sparring (rolling). The warmup usually consists of cardiovascular exercises and BJJ specific moves like shrimps (also referred to as hip escapes), bear crawls, army crawls, front and back rolls as well as basic bodyweight exercises such as pushups, squats, burpees, etc. A good warm up can sometimes feel like a workout in and of itself. The warm up is sometimes followed by stretching. Then the training session typically involves drilling BJJ techniques where you watch an instructor demonstrate a technique, then partner up and practice the technique on a willing partner. Finally there is live sparring which is called rolling in BJJ, and the former willing partner is no longer willing to succumb to the technique, rather now they are trying to control and submit you, as you are him or her. BJJ requires stamina and the ability to apply and withstand pressure. Above all BJJ requires mental toughness as training can be grueling and exhausting. The more grueling the training, the better you become physically and mentally, and the more prepared you are to test your skills in competition.

Training always should be harder than competition. The mental advantage of training physically hard is that you gain confidence in your ability before a competition. Confidence is a key ingredient to success. Confidence enables championship performance during the competition. Therefore gaining confidence from your training is vital when competing. In life, training can be likened to the day to day tasks you grind through in order to achieve your goal. The harder you grind, the closer you get, and ultimately the achievement of that goal is that much more rewarding. Think about the hardest things you've had to accomplish in life. What kind of rewards do those achievements bring to you? If you're like me the rewards are infinite and can't be put into words because the self-belief and enhanced confidence I receive from achieving difficult tasks is priceless. Whether it's winning a Jiu-Jitsu tournament or a sales award, the feeling is the same. That's why it's important to challenge yourself and allow yourself to rise to the occasion. You won't be able to thank yourself enough when you are in a state of ecstasy from doing what you set out to do. And that state of ecstasy is going to be a source for you to accomplish even more. You can tap into it again and again, recreating it in your mind, feeling the sensation, and watching how it manifests your goals into reality. Winning has a compounding effect. That's why it's often said that "Winning is a habit," because the feeling of accomplishment will create more situations where you can get that same feeling. Eventually, you will want that feeling again and again. This is why "Winning is a habit."

Make mental training part of your routine. Whether it be a competition or a business meeting, as warriors that are "born to brawl" we must spend a lot of time preparing for the event. Most of the time, the preparation will be physical, whether it be training, rehearsing a speech, or role playing a sales presentation. Take some time, preferably at the start of your day, to sit still and clear your mind. The mind is like a computer, and all computers need to be shut down or reset to then be upgraded. To upgrade your mind, you need to be still from time to time. Allow your mind to relax and think of nothing. Focus on nothing but your breathing. Some may call this meditation. Let's just call it relaxing your mind. When your mind is relaxed is the best time to use the visualization techniques we discussed earlier in the book. Only when you are still can you clearly see where you want to go. Give yourself time to relax your mind. Then use the relaxed state to visualize and feel new goals being achieved. Finally, expect the outcome you desire. Mental relaxation and visualization has become an integral part of my training, and it is a part of my regimen and daily routine. I feel it has had a positive impact. If you're not currently doing this, I recommend you make it a part of your training and preparation as well. Regular mental training is often the missing ingredient that can bring you to the next level.

If you have read this book until this point, you most likely respect the concepts presented. Therefore you most likely have not questioned the validity of the ideas presented. However, I recognize that some people will want evidence of these concepts in action, so I'm going to give you a few reasons why these concepts work. In business, the concepts described in this book have helped me as a salesperson to become a top producer in various industries such as advertising, medical devices and pharmaceuticals. I have consistently been in the top 20% of salespeople with every company and product I've sold. I have won the top sales award, called President's Club Award, in two different industries (advertising and pharmaceuticals). Similarly, these concepts have encouraged me to start a business, called F.I.T.E. Fit, a wellness program that incorporates mixed martial arts to inspire healthier living. In addition, the concepts have helped me complete this book. I know firsthand that these concepts will help you in business. The concepts are universal, the variable is how you use them and what you use them for. Not only will they help you in business, but they will help you in life.

Like anything else worth doing, there must be intention and drive when you apply the ideas in this book. That purpose comes from us as individuals. We all, most likely, have something that we can apply the concepts in this book to. Whatever the goal, we must commit to the outcome we want. The sooner we commit to getting the job done, the better. I see firsthand the strong correlation between the fighting arts and business because I am involved in both. I know that the opponent we have to contend with most vigorously is ourselves. If we can gain mastery over ourselves, then mastery over a fight or a business venture becomes secondary. We must train our minds by practicing discipline, and gaining confidence by consistent positive action towards the achievement of our goals. The more we see ourselves doing and completing what we tell ourselves we will do, the more self-respect we gain (self-respect is the most important type of respect we can earn, because it is the only type of respect that really matters). Especially when it is something difficult or something that we don't necessarily want to do, such as going to the gym after a long day at the office or getting up early to go workout, it is that much more important to get it done. If we do it simply because we told ourselves we would, we feel better, and we beat procrastination which strengthens our self-respect. This strength and knowledge of self is what eventually leads to self-mastery. In my opinion, self-mastery removes all obstacles and puts us in the ultimate position to win in life.

Recently I have expanded my training to include other Martial Arts because I want to be a well-rounded Martial

Artist. I am practicing self-mastery in all aspect of life. Therefore, I have practiced some striking arts along with other grappling arts besides BJJ. On a trip to Thailand, I participated in a strict Muay Thai class and experienced the extreme conditioning involved in that fighting art. I witnessed serious Muay Thai athletes training and was able to see firsthand their remarkable work ethic. The fitness level of a Muay Thai athlete is extraordinary, as a typical training session involves running, stretching, squats, burpees, pushups, hitting pads, sparring, and more...And the serious Muay Thai athlete trains two or three times per day (not to mention that a lot of them are cigarette smokers, something I found quite paradoxical)! The same level of indoctrination could be said for boxers or any other serious martial artists that train to compete on a regular basis. What practicing other martial arts has helped me to realize is that in order to be competitive in your respective art, you must be consistent and dedicated. It doesn't matter what discipline you choose, they all take consistent effort. There is no other way to put it, serious fighters train hard.

With that being said, consistency and maximum effort also apply to business and other aspects of life. Serious business people work hard. There is no substitute for hard work in the pursuit of your passion. Being well-rounded in business means spending time learning new approaches, techniques and thought patterns. In business you should be educating yourself on your product or service as well as your competitor's products and services. You always can learn from others. Professional fighters watch hours of video of their fights as well as watching their opponents' fights. They are looking for ways to refine technique and be more effective. If you want to do well in business, you must do the same thing, refine your technique and be more effective. There are countless business seminars, and thought leaders willing to share knowledge. Seek them out and spend some time learning from them. There is so much information out there on-line and a lot of it is available for free. Schedule some time and dedicate it to learning. Watch and learn from the best. I am reminded of a saying by one of the greatest salesmen ever, Zig Ziglar: "Motivation is not permanent, neither is showering, that's why I recommend it daily!" Most importantly, find your drive and use it to push you when you don't feel like doing what you know deep down is necessary. If you don't feel like making that extra call or sending that extra email, or finishing that report, remember why you're doing it in the first place. I used to have a picture of my daughter on my desk when I first started in sales and that was all the motivation I needed to make that extra call and land that appointment. I would sit by the phone, sometimes dreading the next sales call, but taking a look at that photo to get a quick spike of adrenaline from the motivation. That little spike of motivation made it a little easier each time to make that call. Then I got good at it, through repetition and trial and error. I began to apply sales techniques with better efficiency and land more appointments, which led to more sales. More sales became more incentive to keep making those sales calls. That type of motivation, although it was sparked by that picture of my daughter, it comes from within us and it will provide the energy to make the extra effort. It's always the little extra that pays off, so make putting in that extra effort something that you do consistently. Make it a habit of yours.

Take managing your time seriously. I feel that with all the goals I set out to accomplish I must schedule my time. With all the distractions, especially with today's technology, I have to stay focused on the task at hand. I feel it is okay to have several goals in life. My priorities primarily lie within my family, business, and the sport I love, BJJ. As I focus on one priority, the others take a back seat as I must focus on one thing at a time. Therefore I must schedule my time and dedicate it to the task at hand and I am fanatical about keeping a calendar. I schedule my time in blocks daily and throughout the week where I am spending a few hours at a time either working on a project, working with a client, training, or spending time with family and friends. I even schedule my rest and recovery time. During my rest and recovery time is when I usually take time to read or watch Jiu-Jitsu instructional videos and combat sports. I feel that having a calendar system where time is blocked off has helped me efficiently progress toward my goals. I waste as little time as possible using a calendar because once I put it in calendar it becomes "real" to me. I know that it must get done. There are times when I put something in my calendar that I don't really want to do, but I know it has to be done, maybe it's an administrative task, or a workout that I know I need to get done, and as soon as I see it in my calendar there is no hiding from it. I just have to do it. Using this system has helped me beat procrastination and achieve more with my time. I encourage you to do the same. Keep a calendar and schedule your days, weeks, months, even years ahead of time. You will accomplish way more than those who are drifting day to day with no direction. Do yourself a huge favor and give your life the direction it deserves. Schedule your time in a calendar.

Don't aspire to be comfortable. There is no comfort zone if you want to be successful. The comfort zone is an illusion and a trap. Remember you were born to brawl, you are a fighter. We all have it in us, but we have to work on cultivating that fighting spirit. It's up to us to get the most out of our ability, and our situation, with the tools that we are given. No matter where we are, we can accomplish way more, and go way further than wherever we are, right now. We can always improve our current situation, but we must fight for it! Professionals do what others won't do, and that's what makes them professionals. If you want to be at the top of your game, you have to train like pro, and do what you were born to do. Attack every day like a fighter ready to brawl!

Enjoy the Journey – Key Points:

- Make a commitment. When you fully commit you give yourself no alternatives. "The absence of alternatives clears the mind absolutely."
- Commitment leads to preparation. Preparation leads to expectation. Expectation leads to success.
- Training should be way harder than competition. Go out of your way to make your training difficult. This will give you the confidence to know that you can handle whatever comes your way during competition.
- Make mental training part of your routine. Take time to sit, breathe, and relax. In a relaxed state you can visualize what you want to happen.
- Winning is a habit. Once you taste victory, you can draw on that feeling to create more victories.
- It's always the little extra effort that pays off. Whether it's an extra rep in the gym, an extra sales call, or an extra word of encouragement to your spouse, make doing more than you set out to do a regular habit. Little extras, over time, pay big dividends.
- Schedule your time. Keep a calendar with daily, weekly, and monthly tasks broken down into blocks of time. Accomplish more with the time you have.

Conclusion

I had a fantastic time interviewing the fighters in this book. Not only are they great fighters but they are phenomenal human beings. My time spent with these fighters was extremely insightful for me and I learned firsthand what separates these elite athletes from their peers as this pertains to all aspects of life. I thoroughly enjoyed learning how these fighters prepare for a fight and their rituals, their characteristics, and traits they employ to help them achieve their goals.

One common thread you may have noticed while reading is that among all the fighters, the concept of preparation was prevalent. Preparation was at the forefront of all the conversations I held with every fighter to whom I spoke. That preparation was not only physical preparation, but also mental preparation. Each fighter takes his preparation extremely seriously. Not only preparing but preparing the right way is an important factor. For most of these fighters preparation is a matter of working on your weaknesses and seeking help when needed. Although the fight itself is an individual event, the preparation is often a team activity. As a fighter, you have training partners, coaches, and supportive friends and family that help you along the way. The preparation with the team and training is where most of the hard work is done. The actual event is the pinnacle of all the effort it took to get to that specific moment. It is where you get to shine and have fun doing what you prepared for. That is the power of preparation. It allows you to enjoy the process, and have fun on the day of the event. Whether you are getting ready for a fight or a business meeting, preparation is the most important element in determining the outcome of the event.

Another common factor in success for these fighters is hard work. This may seem obvious, however, all the fighters had the "love" for what they do combined with hard work. The fighters interviewed had an inherent passion for their craft, although, talent never really was a factor in why they were good at their profession. Regardless of talent, they all attributed hard work to their success. There is no substitute for putting in the consistent hours in training. Even though there will be good and bad days during training, the consistent effort will reward you in the long run. The grind has to be embraced, and the work must be done. It is the most controllable variable in the fight. You can't determine what others do, or what the weather will be, or how others think, but you can control your own effort. You can work hard at the task at hand and train with the intent of putting out maximum effort on event day. You don't reach maximum effort without training to push your limits. "You fight how you train" is a quote often heard in combat sports. I believe it's true. The habits you develop during training will be magnified on fight day. Train hard to make those habits GOOD habits.

Learning from mistakes was often heard in the interviews with these fighters. I can't overstate the humility that these fighters have cultivated. Without humility, there is no learning with an open heart and becoming better. These fighters have embraced failure as part of the process. In martial arts there is the elusive yet constant pursuit of perfection. We martial artists are fanatical about mastery, as we perform technique after technique, until it becomes muscle memory, and then we find ways to perfect it even more. It never ends. That is the process of learning. It should never end. Your achievements and losses today teach you how to strive for tomorrow's success. Embrace the mistakes, learn from them, and be your own comparison. Progress is personal and you can only judge it yourself. You know what kind of effort you have been putting in, and how much work you are doing to improve your weaknesses. Learning gives you the knowledge and it is up to you to apply the knowledge. You can achieve tremendous growth, and it is your responsibility to self-assess and make sure that you are growing. Keeping a journal is a great way to self-assess and make sure that we are moving toward the achievement of our goals. A good journal with consistent notes will give you cues on what is working and what needs work. You can then apply what is working with more diligence and modify what is not working. This is true learning.

I wish you much success as a "Born Brawler." Your inherent fighting spirit will take you far if you let it. Cultivate discipline by following the guidelines in this book. These concepts and ideas are intended to help you when you start to create your own guidelines. You can come back to this book as a reference and as a way to hold yourself accountable. Start with one approach at time. The fighters in each chapter present several key points for you to follow. Go to the chapters and points that you find the most relatable first. Then expand to other key points and start applying those in your life. You will find that the order you follow is what you most likely need at that point in time. I also encourage you to add to the list of key points that help you most. Please take the time to advance your learning by reading books, listening to books, and watching educational videos on your craft, profession, or art. You will add to the key points, traits, and characteristics that will give you the fighter's edge. There is much more that can be added, and in writing this book I expected this to be as such. I know that learning is eternal, and I devised this book to be a good teacher by inspiring a desire for more learning. Your constant development is what will fuel your growth and subsequent success. Never stop reaching for your next level, and always keep brawling!

End Notes

Chapter 4

[1] I actually read the same book as Leo, in which the author explains the technique Leo described where he gave himself 10 minutes to vent after a loss, then mentally moved on after the 10 minutes was up. The book is called "The Art of Mental Training" by DC Gonzales.

Chapter 8

[2] Since this interview Formiga separated his association with Soul Fighters Jiu-Jitsu, and now continues to spread the Jiu-Jitsu lifestyle through a new organization called Double Five Jiu-Jitsu. Leonardo Delgado who was interviewed in chapter 4 has joined Formiga and is also currently associated with Double Five Jiu-Jitsu.

ABOUT THE AUTHOR

Julian Rivera is an entrepreneur, an accomplished professional sales person, an author, a musician, and a Brazilian Jiu-Jitsu Black Belt registered with the International Brazilian Jiu-Jitsu Federation (IBJJF). His passions all require self-learning, and he thrives on knowledge and its practical application. His core belief is that every day is an opportunity to get better. His vision is that he will empower others to achieve their goals through his creativity and teachings.

Julian trains and competes regularly in Martial Arts tournaments as he thoroughly enjoys Martial Arts and Self-Defense. Julian's awards in competition include IBJJF No-Gi Gold Medalist as a Brown Belt, and IBJJF Pan Am No-Gi Silver Medalist as a Black Belt. Julian's passion for Martial Arts has inspired him to live a healthy lifestyle and he knows that Martial Arts has the potential do the same for others. This is the motivation behind what he does, including his book(s).

Julian Rivera has thrived and succeeded as a professional sales leader within the most multifaceted industries. These industries include Advertising, Information Technology, and Healthcare. These industries provided the education where he was able to fine tune his skills during his sales career. He has helped companies such as Yellowbook USA (now Hibu), Modis, Fisher & Paykel Healthcare, and Horizon Therapeutics gain significant market share by exponentially increasing new and existing business. As a sales person, Julian has been awarded the highest sales achievement award in multiple industries. He won the President's Club Circle of Achievement Award with Yellow Book USA, and the President's Club Circle of Achievement Award with Horizon Therapeutics.

In August of 2017 Julian started a Corporate Wellness Company by the name of F.I.T.E. Fit, which is a martial arts based fitness program that incorporates self-defense. As a dedicated martial artist, he decided to take that passion and combine it with an emerging industry, corporate wellness. F.I.T.E. Fit is a company that has a network of trainers with specialties and certifications in Fitness, Self-Defense, Martial Arts, Women's Self-Defense, Nutrition, Mobility training, Weapons training, and CPR training. Julian leverages his network of professionals to customize programs for companies and organizations depending on their wellness needs and goals. F.I.T.E. Fit uses martial arts to encourage healthier living. Julian hosts a YouTube channel, Facebook page, and Instagram profile for F.I.T.E. Fit where he posts helpful tips, techniques, and advice for martial artists, fitness enthusiasts, and people who want to stay healthy. https://www.youtube.com/channel/UCTOcgf_A_wn6yaevwWZdDTA https://www.facebook.com/fit2fite https://www.instagram.com/fitefit1/

In addition to professional selling, entrepreneurship, training martial arts, and competing, Julian is also a musician. He makes walk out music for MMA fighters under the artist name Paradox BX. He has made walk out tracks for Johnny Lopez, Roberto Rios, Matt Bessette, Justin Valentin, David Michael Durao, and other MMA fighters. Julian hosts a YouTube channel and Facebook page for his music under the name Paradox BX:

https://www.youtube.com/channel/UCUUIy-YdFD1qTVjA1O5WVLw
https://www.facebook.com/paradoxproducts

In "Born to Brawl: Gaining a Fighter's Edge in Business and Life," Julian utilized his network of champion caliber fighters to compose a book which will help people reach their business and life goals. Julian believes that anyone can use the same principles these fighters use to earn massive accomplishments. As an author he intends to create books that are in line with his vision. “Born to Brawl: Gaining a Fighter’s Edge in Business and Life” is Julian’s first book.

Made in the USA
Columbia, SC
09 November 2020

24230149R00074